WEIRD BRITISH COLUMBIA LAWS

Strange, Bizarre, Wacky & Absurd

WEIRD BRITISH COLUMBIA LAWS

Strange, Bizarre, Wacky & Absurd

Mark Thorburn

BLUE
BIKE
BOOKS

The Publisher: Blue Bike Books
Website: www.bluebikebooks.com

Library and Archives Canada Cataloguing in Publication

Thorburn, Mark, 1958–
        Weird British Columbia laws / Mark Thornburn.

ISBN 978-1-926700-01-4

        1. Law—British Columbia—Humor. 2. Law—British
Columbia—Popular works.
I. Title.

K184.7.C2T46 2011   349.71102'07   C2010-907620-6

Project Director: Nicholle Carrière
Project Editor: Wendy Pirk
Cover Image: Roger Garcia
Illustrations: Peter Tyler, Roger Garcia, Patrick Hénaff, Djorde Todorovic,
Roly Wood, Graham Johnson

We acknowledge the support of the Alberta Foundation for the Arts for
our publishing program.
We acknowledge the financial support of the Government of Canada
through the Canada Book Fund (CBF) for our publishing activities.

DEDICATION

To my three favourite lawbreakers, Joseph, Albert and Jules, and to Albert's pet snake, Adolphe.

ACKNOWLEDGEMENTS

Thank you to Blue Bike Books and Nicholle Carrière for the opportunity to work on this project. I really appreciate it!

And many thanks to my editor, Wendy Pirk, whose patience, skill and marvellous insights contributed significantly to this book.

CONTENTS

PROPER PUBLIC ATTIRE (OR LACK THEREOF)

CRIME

HOUSE AND HOME

FOREIGNERS

TAXES

VOTING

COLONIAL BC

MISCELLANEOUS

INTRODUCTION

When I was a teenager in Santa Clara County, California, in the early 1970s, one of the local municipalities considered a bylaw to outlaw rain on Sundays. (I don't recall if the measure was actually adopted or not.) Another nearby community set the speed limits in its residential areas not in five-mile increments, but at 17 and 21 miles per hour. But after many years of being an attorney and legal historian, these are the only laws I know of that were weird from the beginning.

Rarely do lawmakers vote for a bylaw, ordinance or statute with the intention of making themselves look silly. Virtually every law is enacted either to address some problem or threat (real or perceived) or to enforce or try to instill rules of conduct held dear by those who hold political power. It is the passage of time and changes in attitudes, culture and society in general that turn old statutes and bylaws into oddities that we can laugh at today.

For example, Vancouver once approved a bylaw that required all public bathers, men and women alike, to be dressed from neck to ankle. It may seem silly now (and the fact that it was not repealed until 1986 may make it seem even sillier), but it was perfectly natural in 1896 in light of Victorian propriety at the time.

Victoria once set a city-wide speed limit of only 6 miles (10 kilometres) per hour. A bit odd in today's age of mechanized vehicles, but it made sense in 1873 when there was not yet any cars in the province and the horse buggy and bicycle were still the primary means of in-town transportation.

Other old statutes and bylaws are weird by today's standards not because they strike our funny bone, but because they would be considered odd or bizarre and raise an eyebrow, if not some concern about our constitutional rights, if they were in force today.

For instance, BC is now populated by people of many faiths and has not only churches of various denominations, but also synagogues, mosques, temples, gudwaras and other places of worship. So it might be surprising to learn that until only a few years ago (i.e., 1989) a provincial law required all public schools in BC to begin the day with a reading from the Christian Holy Scripture and a recitation of the Lord's Prayer.

Today's box office hits include *No Strings Attached* (about a couple involved in non-marital sex), the Coen brothers' *True Grit* (which depicts shootings, hangings and the chopping off of fingers) and *The King's Speech* (with its focus on King George VI's stutter and its unflattering portrayal of authority figures such as Edward VIII and the Archbishop of Canterbury, Cosmo Lang). British Columbians would be out-raged if the province still had a censor who could ban these movies, or at least require major alterations, just as he prohib-ited innocuous films such as *Abbott and Costello Meet Frankenstein* from BC's movie theatres for over five decades.

Just over 40 percent of Richmond's residents, as well as almost 30 percent of Vancouverites and about 10 percent of all British Columbians, are of Chinese descent. But the prov-ince once had a statute that banned Chinese Canadians from voting and another that prohibited Caucasian women from being employed at, or even frequenting as customers, any business run by a Chinese Canadian.

When discussing weird BC laws, it might be helpful to remember a few things. First, like most other English-speaking jurisdictions, BC's law is based on English common law. This law is the result of centuries of court decisions and precedent and is typically adhered to except when a statute or bylaw has altered it. If there is no statute or bylaw, then the common law still governs even if it is centuries old.

Second, the colonies of Vancouver Island and mainland British Columbia each inherited England's common and statutory law as those laws existed at the date of the colonies' creation, 1849 for Vancouver Island and 1858 for the mainland. Much of the common law is still the law today in BC. Furthermore, many of those statutes remained intact for decades in BC until the provincial legislature changed them, and some of those laws were not altered until long after the Brits themselves had repealed or altered the originals.

Third, because of its size, Vancouver has a preponderance of weird municipal bylaws. The city was incorporated in 1886, but within 25 years it was home to over 100,000 residents, a figure that represented more than one-quarter of the province's entire population. It was not until 1961 that another municipality in BC, Burnaby, had as many inhabitants.

And until the mid-20th century, most of what are today British Columbia's largest cities were small, rural communities. In 1921, for example, only five other cities in BC besides Vancouver had more than 10,000 residents (Victoria, 38,700; South Vancouver, 32,200; New Westminster, 14,500; Point Grey, 13,700; and Burnaby, 12,900). As a result, many issues that Vancouver faced, and would adopt bylaws on, were never encountered by BC's smaller communities.

It should also be noted that Vancouver is unique in that it has a city charter, granted to it by the BC government, which gives its council the right to set laws and regulations on a large variety of matters that, elsewhere, are within the exclusive jurisdiction of the province.

Laws often reflect the attitudes, concerns and fears of a particular time in history. For example, considering the hundreds of thousands of people who swamped downtown Vancouver during the 2010 Olympics, it is ironic that, 100 years before, the city's fathers were so afraid of the union movement that they prohibited gatherings of more than three people. Or that, with women involved now as equals in business and politics, they were denied in the 19th century not only the vote, but also the right to control their own property or have a say in the raising of their children.

Finally, there have been federal laws that have had a peculiar, if not unique, effect upon British Columbians. For instance, one statute adopted by Ottawa outlawed the potlatch, a cultural event that is important to many of BC's Natives. Another, aimed at preventing obscene books from entering Canada, resulted in a police raid at the Vancouver Public Library and led the Victoria Library to hide a novel from the authorities.

This book contains weird laws, municipal bylaws, provincial statutes and regulations, and federal legislation that have all affected British Columbians. Some will make you chuckle; others will cause you to scratch your head and wonder. Hopefully, all will entertain.

Enjoy!

Driving

*Public safety on the roads has always been a high priority
for municipalities and the provincial government.
But the laws as to whom could be on the street, at what
speed and under what circumstances have had some
bizarre results....*

SPEED LIMITS
In the Beginning…

In 1873, the Victoria City Council set the first speed
limit in British Columbia at an astonishing 6 miles (10 kilometres) per hour! Cars did not yet exist, but the restriction
applied to bicycles, horses and all other non-motorized
forms of transportation.

Watch Your Speed

The first BC statute to deal with cars was the Motor Vehicle
Speed Regulation Act of 1904. Among other things, this law
set province-wide speed limits at 10 miles (16 kilometres) per
hour in cities, towns and incorporated villages and 15 miles
(24 kilometres) per hour everywhere else. Going any faster
could cost you a fine of up to $25 (almost $600 today) and,
starting with your second offence, up to one month in jail!

You're Going too Fast!
Province-wide speed limits were increased in 1911 to
10 miles (16 kilometres) per hour in cities, towns and
villages, 25 miles (40 kilometres) per hour in "open
country" and 12 (yes, 12!) miles (19 kilometres) per hour in
"wooded country." You also could not go faster than 4 miles
(6 kilometres) per hour when passing a stationary streetcar
that was dropping off or picking up passengers. And you
could not approach or pass within 100 yards (90 metres)
of any horse or horse-drawn vehicle at a speed faster than
10 miles (16 kilometres) per hour. Speeding tickets could
now cost you up to $300 (that's $7200 today!) and, if you
couldn't pay, up to six months imprisonment.

A Nice, Slow Drive Through the Park
The Vancouver Park Board decreed in 1906 that no
automobile could be driven through Stanley Park between

2:00 and 5:00 PM on Saturday and Sunday afternoons. It also decided that the speed limit in any city park (applicable to horses, bikes and animal-driven carriages as well as to cars and all other vehicles) was a speedy 8 miles (13 kilometres) per hour.

CASE FILE
I Wasn't Going that Fast!

A man was arrested in Surrey on April 20, 1910, for speeding in his 1907 Marion. He was going 12 miles (19 kilometres) per hour in a 10-mile (16 kilometres) zone, and his lead foot cost him $10 (about $225 today) plus $2.50 in court costs!

Slow Down at Intersections

A 1919 Vancouver bylaw set the speed limit throughout the city for bicycles, motorcycles, cars, horses and horse-drawn vehicles at 15 miles (24 kilometres) per hour. At street intersections, however, everyone had to slow down to 6 miles (10 kilometres) per hour.

Go Slow on that Bridge!

The BC Legislative Assembly in 1905 passed a law making it illegal to ride or drive any animal or animals at a pace faster than a walk over a bridge owned or supervised by the provincial government. The same act also forbade anyone from mooring or in any way attaching any raft, boat, vessel or anything else that floats to such a bridge. To do so would have cost you a fine of up to $50, a month in jail and liability for any damages to the structure.

A Forgotten Bylaw

Just over a decade ago, hundreds if not thousands of cyclists in Delta in the early 2000s violated a local bylaw and didn't even know it.

Canada's largest cycling race, the Tour de Delta, has been held in Delta every year since 2001. However, the local municipal council passed a bylaw in 1898 making it illegal to ride a bicycle faster than 8 miles (13 kilometres) per hour on any of the city's public streets. You also couldn't go any faster than 5 miles (8 kilometres) per hour when turning corners. And the same bylaw required all bike riders to stay on the left side of the road and to sound a warning bell whenever they approached an intersection.

Originally, violators were subject to a fine of up to $3 for their first offence and up to $10 for every offence afterward. But everyone had forgotten about the bylaw by the time the first Tour de Delta was held, and it was not repealed until someone discovered it in 2004.

LICENCE AND REGISTRATION, PLEASE

All Cars Must Be Registered!

The first automobile in British Columbia was a Stanley Steamer that was purchased and brought to Vancouver by William Henry Armstrong in 1898 (some sources say 1899). By 1907, there were 175 cars in the province.

The Motor Vehicle Speed Regulation Act of 1904 required all automobile owners to register their vehicles with the Superintendent of Provincial Police. A one-time registration fee of $2 (or almost $50 in today's money) was charged, but it was increased in 1911 to $10 and became payable every year.

A Chauffeur by Any Other Name...

Beginning in 1911, all commercial drivers in BC, including truck and taxicab operators, were "chauffeurs" under the law. To be a "chauffeur" required a yearly $5 licence. You had to be at least 17 years old to apply for the licence as well as provide the names and addresses of two character witnesses. The applicant also needed to prove to the cops that he or she was fit and capable "to act as a chauffeur," though the law did not specify how this was to be done.

Starting in 1920, all chauffeurs had to wear a government-issued badge on their hat or cap. (That was later changed to wearing the badge on any conspicuous part of their clothing.)

And beginning in 1925, chauffeurs had to be at least 21 to drive a motor vehicle carrying passengers, but they could be younger if they had permission from the Superintendent of Motor Vehicles. How one got this permission was not specified in the statute.

I Can Drive!

BC's Motor Vehicle Act was changed in 1925 to require all drivers, not just chauffeurs, to have a licence. A licence cost $1 (or about $12 in today's money) and was good for the lifetime of the driver, but even then people thought it was just a money grab by the government. It wasn't until 1932 that you had to renew your licence on a regular basis. (Back then, it was once a year.)

The First Driver's Test

Beginning in 1925, all you had to do to get either a chauffeur's or a regular driver's licence was to prove that you could read and understand road signs and traffic signals. The law was changed in 1939 to require you to pass a road test and prove that you could actually drive.

What Colour Is Your Licence?

Drivers' licences in 1935 came in three colours: white, blue and yellow.

Everyone started with a licence printed on white paper. If convicted of a traffic offence, a driver might be required by the judge to turn over the white licence in exchange for a blue one. If convicted of another traffic offence while holding a blue licence, then the offender had to surrender it for a yellow one. And if convicted of yet another traffic offence...well, that's it—you lost your privilege to drive altogether.

The judge could suspend or cancel your driving privileges upon your first two convictions if your actions warranted it, but the Commissioner of Provincial Police (whose office was then in charge of issuing drivers' licences) could overturn the decision and issue the blue or yellow licence instead. And if you didn't commit another traffic offence for at least one year, you could go to the commissioner to trade in your yellow licence for a blue one or your blue licence for white.

Granted, computers did not yet exist, but you'd think they could have found a better way to keep track of your driving record!

PARKING BYLAWS

Parking Your Horse

Vancouver's city council made it illegal in 1919 to park your car, or to allow your horse or other animal to be left standing, for more than 10 minutes between 7:00 AM and 7:00 PM on most of the city's downtown streets. The 10 minutes was expanded to a half hour in 1920, but only along those parts of a street where no streetcar tracks had been laid.

The Right Angle

A 1920 Vancouver bylaw required that, when leaving your horse or car on Granville Street between Burrard and Hamilton, you had to "stand" the animal or vehicle at a 45-degree angle to the centre of the street. Also, if you left your horse or car on Burrard Street between Robson and Hastings, then you had to "stand" them at a right angle (i.e., 90 degrees) to the centre of the street.

Red Lights on Street

A 1930 bylaw in the Township of Langley made it illegal "during the period from one-half hour after sunset to one-half hour before sunrise" to park your car on any street without attaching a lighted red lamp to the back of the vehicle that could be seen for a distance of at least 50 feet (15 metres).

The same bylaw made it unlawful to drive any wagon, carriage or other vehicle drawn by an animal on any street between sunset and sunrise unless there was one lighted white lamp attached to the front of the vehicle and a red one to the rear. Both of these also had to be seen from at least 50 feet (15 metres).

THE SOUNDS THAT VEHICLES MAKE

Don't Frighten the Horse

A 1904 statute mandated that any car, when approaching a horse-drawn vehicle or any horse that was ridden or otherwise under somebody's control, had to exercise "every reasonable precaution" not to frighten the animal. If the horse was scared, then the car driver had to slow down, and even stop if requested by the horse's handler, until the animal calmed down.

Apparently horses don't like the sounds that automobiles make. The statute was amended in 1911 so that if a horse's handler asked you to stop, you had to turn off your engine, too!

Honk the Horn

The 1904 Motor Vehicle Speed Regulation Act required every automobile in the province to be equipped with an alarm bell, gong or horn that was suppose to be sounded "whenever it shall be reasonably necessary to be sounded" (now that makes a lot of sense!) to notify "pedestrians and others" of the vehicle's approach. It didn't matter whether the pedestrians were crossing the street or just walking along the sidewalk. Presumably the "others" were other automobiles, horse-drawn vehicles and anything else that was on the road.

The Noise, the Noise, Noise, Noise!

Vancouver's streets sure must have been noisy after 1919! A city bylaw adopted that year required all bicycles and cars to have a bell, gong, horn or whistle, and their drivers had to sound these instruments whenever "approaching any streetcar, vehicle, horse or other animal or pedestrian." It didn't matter if you were approaching the traffic or were passing from behind. It also didn't matter if the pedestrian was merely walking on the sidewalk or about to cross the street.

The regulation also required all bike and car drivers to sound their devices when "approaching any place where any person may be entering or leaving any streetcar, or other public conveyance, or upon approaching any street intersection, or before passing any street corner" whether or not anyone was in the intersection or on the street corner.

RULES OF THE ROAD
In a One-horse Open Sleigh

The Yale Cariboo Road (aka the Yale-Cariboo Trunk Road or the "second" Cariboo Wagon Road) operated from 1865 to 1885. It started in Yale and went north through the Fraser Canyon, past Hell's Gate and Jackass Mountain, through Lytton and Ashcroft, and on to Clinton where it hooked up with the "first" Cariboo Wagon Road (which was built in 1861). From there the road continued on to the Cariboo Gold Fields.

The road was primarily used by stagecoaches and freight wagon companies that were headquartered at Yale, but sleighs also travelled on it during winter. Apparently too many top-heavy sleighs tipped over and lost their cargo because, in 1883, the Legislative Assembly adopted a law requiring all sleighs carrying freight on the road "to be of a width of not less than three feet six inches [106 centimetres] from centre to centre of runners." Violators faced a fine of between $10 and $25 (or roughly between $225 and $565 in today's money) and possible imprisonment of up to 21 days.

The provincial legislature amended the law in 1884 to exempt the stretch from Stanley (now a ghost town east of Quesnel) to Barkerville.

Plank Roads

Dirt roads and bridges covered with a series of wooden planks were very common in British Columbia before the introduction of asphalt in the 1920s. However, heavy vehicles could wreck havoc on them, so the Township of Langley adopted a bylaw in 1900 prohibiting any "mode of conveyance" weighing more than 6000 pounds (2722 kilograms) from being "driven or otherwise propelled upon or over any of the plank roads or bridges" within the municipality. Violators faced a fine of up to $50 or three months in jail. There was a loophole: the prohibition did not apply if the owner or the person in charge of the "mode of conveyance" furnished and laid down on the road or bridge additional planks "of sufficient strength and thickness" to protect the original planks from damage.

TRAFFIC ODDS AND ENDS

You're Too Young to Drive!

British Columbia initially allowed anyone, regardless of age, to drive motorized vehicles, including commercial trucks and taxis. The first minimum age requirement was set at 17 by the Motor Traffic Regulation Act of 1911. It was raised to 21 in 1932, but if you were over 16 you could still get a driver's permit provided you had your parents' written consent and you proved to the local police that you were a "fit and competent person" to drive. How you did the latter was not specified in the statute.

Don't Drink and Drive

The 1911 statute also made it illegal to drive while "under [the] influence of intoxicating liquor." No specific blood-alcohol level or other method of determining drunkenness was specified in the law, but driving while under the influence could result in a ticket of up to $300 or up to six months in jail.

Don't Idle

A 2009 bylaw has made illegal in Tofino for a person to idle a vehicle for more than three consecutive minutes. However, there are a number of exceptions, including emergency vehicles, cars that are stuck in traffic or that pick up or drop off passengers, or vehicles participating in parades.

No More Fancy Motorcycling
It became illegal in 1925 for any person to drive or otherwise operate a motorcycle without their tail end in the driver's seat.

Tricycles

Most tricycles are ridden by tiny tots whom you don't want in the middle of a street, but a 1929 bylaw in the Township of Langley made it illegal to ride trikes on the one safe place that we're accustomed to seeing them: the sidewalk. No exceptions were made for youngsters or those accompanied by a parent.

Furthermore, everyone who rode a tricycle at night had to attach a light on the front of their vehicle and a reflector or a light on the back, and both had to be visible from a distance of at least 50 feet (15 metres).

Watch out kiddies! The penalty for violating the bylaw was a fine of up to $100 (about $1240 today!) or up to two months in jail.

How Do You Embarrass a Car?
The Township of Langley in 1914 made it unlawful to engage "in any sport, amusement, exercise or occupation likely or calculated to frighten horses or embarrass or delay the passage of vehicles." The dictionary says that one of the definitions of "embarrass" is "to hamper or impede."

Driving on the Wrong Side of the Road

Drivers in British Columbia drove on the left side of the road until 2:00 AM on January 1, 1922, when a provincial statute required everyone to switch to the right.

Show Respect for the Dead

A 1911 BC statute required the driver of any motorized vehicle on any highway, street or road "outside of the limits of a city" to stop and, when able, pull off onto an intersecting road whenever they came upon a funeral procession and to wait until the motorcade had passed.

You Can't Take My Taxi

Vancouver's city fathers did not look kindly upon "notoriously bad characters" and "women of ill-fame." An 1886 bylaw prohibited cab drivers from providing transportation to such people within the city during the daytime unless it was to take them "to or from the railway station, or wharf or steam-boat landing." Tree Huggers and Plant Lovers

The Natural World

Trees, shrubs and even the lowly weed have been the subject of government regulation. Some of the statutes and bylaws that have been adopted, whether to protect the plants or eradicate them, are certainly odd.

TREE HUGGERS AND PLANT LOVERS

Protect the Tree!

The Township of Langley in 1914 made it illegal to tie or fasten a horse to any tree located in a public place. You also couldn't climb the tree or place any handbill or placard on it.

Save the Cascara!

Rhamnus purshiana, more commonly known as the cascara tree, grows about 10 metres high and has greyish black bark, oblong leaves, greenish flowers and purplish black berries. Extract from its bark and wood is used as flavouring in liquors, non-alcoholic drinks and ice cream and has been used as a laxative for over 1000 years.

Found throughout most of Vancouver Island, the southern coast of the Lower Mainland and the Columbia Valley, the tree must have been particularly important to the residents of the Township of Langley. Their town council enacted a bylaw in 1941 making it illegal to dig up, cut down, injure, deface or destroy "in part or in whole" any cascara tree found in a park or on other municipal property, or on private property, without the prior consent of the property owner. Violators faced up to $50 in fines and one month in jail.

Tree Hugging at Its Finest
You can cut trees in the district of Hope. Well, sometimes you can. The community's 1995 tree protection bylaw makes it clear that anyone who wants to cut down a tree must get a permit first. However, you'll only get a permit if your request follows some specific regulations. Among other things, you have to provide the city's municipal engineer with a letter explaining why you need to cut the tree, a tree survey and proof of liability insurance carried by the tree-removal company hired for the job.

CONTROL THE PESKY PLANTS

Trim Those Trees

Out-of-control greenery encroaching on town sidewalks or on public roadways is against the law in Oak Bay. In 1994, the town council made it law for residents to control their foliage with a Hazardous Tree and Shrub Bylaw.

Get Your Weeders Out

What can you say that's nice about noxious weeds? There were so many of them along the roadsides of Surrey in 1891 that a bylaw was passed to get rid of them. Workers were paid $2 per day to get the job done.

What Are You Doing on June 20?

The *Cirsium arvense*, aka the Canadian thistle, is an ugly little green plant that, if allowed to grow, will produce a pinkish-purple flower. Most regard it as a noxious weed. So noxious in fact that the Township of Langley passed a bylaw in 1914 requiring all owners and occupiers of land to cut the plant three times a year to within 5 centimetres of the ground to destroy all Canadian thistles on their land. Otherwise, the township would cut the area down and send the owners the bill. And when was the Canadian thistle to be cut down? On or before June 20, July 20 and August 13 of each year.

Animals

Just as some old laws dealing with people and their behaviour seem weird today, there have also been rules and regulations regarding our winged and four-footed friends that appear equally strange. Let's have a look.

NO LOITERING!
Oink, Oink, Baaaaaa

So many pigs and goats were roaming free on public streets and getting into people's yards in Victoria's early days that the colonial legislature had to step in and do something about it. So, in 1862, it passed a statute making it "unlawful for the owners of Swine, Goats and Kids, to suffer them to be at large within the limits of the Town of Victoria, and to suffer Goats and Kids to be at large within any of the settled Districts of Vancouver Island."

Any pigs or goats found at large would be considered "trespassers" and could be shot on sight by police. A land-owner also had the right to shoot these trespassers if the animals were found on his property. The beasts could even be shot "while escaping" from the landowner's premises! Of course, it was still all right to keep pigs and goats confined "within suitable buildings or enclosures."

I've Arrested a Jackass

Other animals faired a little better under the Breeding Stock Act of 1876. That law made it illegal for any "stallion, jackass, bull, boar or ram" to run at large in any part of British Columbia except the municipalities, which were allowed to have their own bylaws governing the matter, and those parts of the province located north and east of the Cascade Range.

The owner of a roaming beast was subject to a $25 fine (almost $500 today) if the animal was caught. Furthermore, the power to "arrest and detain" the creature was granted to any British Columbian who ran across it while pasturing his own cows, horses, pigs or sheep on his property or on public land.

The cattle rancher (or shepherd or pig farmer or whatever) had to notify the owner of the offending beast when an "arrest" was made and give said owner 10 days to reclaim the animal. If the owner didn't, then the arresting rancher could sell it. The owner was also required to pay the rancher for the animal's care and upkeep: $5 plus 50 cents a day on the first arrest and $10 plus $1 a day on the second. If the offending animal was male and was arrested a third time, the rancher could castrate it and turn it loose provided the surgery was done with "reasonable skill."

In the Good Old Summertime

The Township of Langley in 1921 made it illegal year-round for the owners of various types of animals to allow their pets and livestock to run freely on any public road, street or highway, or to trespass on any unenclosed land, vacant land or public place within the municipality. These animals included horses, bulls, rams, pigs, "breachy" (i.e., unruly) cattle, turkeys, geese, ducks and chickens. Cats and dogs were not on the list.

In contrast, the owners of sheep, as well as those of calm, obedient cattle, could let their animals roam wherever they wanted between April 1 and November 1, as long as the creatures stayed out of a restricted area set out in the bylaw. During the rest of the year, however, the animals were bound by the same rules as the other restricted pets and livestock.

Want to Feed Upon a Road?

Esquimalt adopted a bylaw in 1912 that made it illegal for a large number of animals (horses, cows, sheep, goats, dogs, geese, ducks, etc.) to run at large or trespass within the city limits. It was also unlawful for them "to graze, browse or feed upon any road or roads or unfenced lands" in the municipality. However, cows, calves and sheep were allowed to graze on "vacant spaces," but not on roads, between 6:00 AM and 8:00 PM from April 1 to October 1 and between 7:00 AM and 5:00 PM the rest of the year so long as they were under the control of a herdsman or shepherd.

The penalty charged to the owners of the animals for breaking this bylaw was only $2 if the creature was a horse, ass, mule or a member of the bovine family, but $25 if it was a goose, duck or dog, and $50 (or almost $1100 in today's money) if it was a pig, sheep or goat.

No Mooo in That Town

It is against the law to allow your cattle to roam the streets of Port Coquitlam. If your animal is caught, the local police will tell you to mooo-ve it.

A Dog's Day

The Township of Langley passed a bylaw regarding dogs in 1926. Specifically, they could not "be at large at any time between sunset and sunrise unless accompanied or being within reasonable call of the owner or of some person having the charge or care thereof." Nothing was said in any bylaw at the time about dogs running at large during the day.

Great Wages (and Milk, Too!)
The Township of Langley's pound keeper was highly motivated in 1921 to pick up stray animals. He collected a fee for every animal that was impounded; the exact amount depended on the type of creature, how much time passed before the owners picked up their pet and whether or not the animal had to be sold off at auction if the owners never showed up. The pound keeper got to keep every cent of those fees if he caught the animal himself, but only 50 percent if someone else brought it to him. In addition, if the animal was a "milch" cow, the pound keeper got to keep as much of the milk as he could use and then sell the rest.

Put a Leash on Those Bees

Chetwynd adopted in 1969 a bylaw governing the public's use of its parks and other recreational property.

One of the bylaw's provisions states, "no person shall suffer or allow any bees...owned or controlled by himself to trespass or run at large in any park." Furthermore, all bees—as well as any dogs, poultry or "domesticated birds or insects"—found running at large or trespassing in a city park are subject to seizure, detention and impoundment.

Another paragraph prohibits people from disturbing or frightening any bird or animal in a park. Strict liability applies; no intent is required on the part of the perpetrator to be found guilty of violating the bylaw. Still, it's hard not to scare away the squirrels you meet while strolling along a park trail.

IT'S PUBLIC LAND
A Horse Is a Horse, Unless It's a Cow

A statute enacted by the provincial legislature in 1876 allowed the government, upon the request of two-thirds of the local resident landowners north and east of the Cascade Range, to set aside Crown land for landowners to "depasture" their cattle. This is one of the few laws in the world where "cattle" was defined to include horses and pigs.

In exchange for this pasture land, the cattle owners had to pay the province five cents a year per animal. Finally, no sheep were allowed on any such "common" land except when in transit from one location to another; even then, they were not allowed to stay for more than 24 hours.

Watch Out, Mr. Ed!
According to the Wild Horses Act of 1906, anyone who owned at least five horses that ranged on public land could get a licence from the BC government to shoot all the unbranded horses they found running wild on those same lands. This law, however, applied only to that part of British Columbia located east of the Cascade Range.

BEWARE OF LARGE, FOUR-LEGGED CREATURES

No Animals on Sidewalks or Bridges

A 1914 bylaw made it unlawful in the Township of Langley to lead, ride or "drive" any animal on a sidewalk or to allow it to stand on one. A 1930 bylaw made it illegal to permit a dog or any other animal to stand on a bridge. It was also unlawful to leave an animal attached to a car, bicycle, wagon or other vehicle on any street without it being securely tethered to the vehicle.

Animal Control in Smithers
It is illegal to ride or herd cattle, goats, horses or pigs on Smithers' sidewalks. The walkways are crowded enough with people and their small pets.

Horses Impede Walk to School

Almost 1000 children in Surrey walked to school every day in 1959, many along busy roads, because they lived less than 3 miles (5 kilometres) from their schoolhouse. You see, school buses were available only for those whose homes were farther away. Parents in Surrey asked that the bus service pick up kids who resided between 2 and 3 miles (3 and 5 kilometres) from their school, but that idea was rejected as being too costly. Instead, the city agreed to create gravel footpaths along the streets where vehicular traffic was heavy. But Surrey at that time was also home to about 12,000 horses, and soon horse riders were using these new pathways as bridle paths, crowding out the school children and other pedestrians. So, the Surrey City Council stepped in and passed a bylaw outlawing the use of the pathways by horses.

CASE FILE
No Camels on the Cariboo Road!

The legislature of the mainland colony of British Columbia outlawed the use of camels on the Cariboo Road in 1862. Only four months before the law was instated, Lillooet entrepreneur Frank Laumeister imported 21 of the creatures from California to use as pack animals along the route. Seems that the animals were hard to handle, smelled a lot, ate plenty of soap and clothes, and caused horses, mules and oxen to stampede.

TO HUNT OR NOT TO HUNT

Bounty for Bears and Cougars

An 1881 Surrey bylaw authorized the payment of a bounty for every beast of prey killed within the municipality's borders. Large numbers of bears and cougars were soon being killed for $2.50 each (or about $55 today). The bounty was repealed in 1892, not because there were no bears left, but because so many had been shot that the city was starting to run out of money.

Leave Those Badgers Alone!
Nanaimo adopted a bylaw in 1896 outlawing badger baiting. Apparently somebody there liked these short-legged members of the weasel family.

Can't Kill Ogopogo

An order in council was approved in 1989 under BC's Wildlife Act making it illegal to kill any "animal in Okanagan Lake, other than a sturgeon, that is more than 3 metres in length and the mate or offspring of that animal." In case you're wondering, that's Ogopogo they're talking about.

LIMITS ON ANIMAL POPULATIONS

Too Many Cows!

An 1896 Vancouver bylaw made it illegal for any family, partnership or corporation to keep more than three cows within city limits. The number was increased to 25 in 1901. And starting in 1910, you couldn't keep a cow or a goat within the city unless you first had a permit from the city's medical health officer, a certificate of the animal's good health from a veterinarian, 1000 square feet (93 square metres) of pasture and a stable.

You Can Have Only Four

It's illegal in Port Coquitlam to own more than four pet rats. Any more and ratatouille might no longer be a vegetarian dish in that city.

Are You Chicken?

Most municipalities have bylaws prohibiting urban poultry. However, while it bans the keeping of roosters and other "farm animals," Victoria allows residents to keep hens as pets. Apparently there's no limit on the number. Nearby Esquimalt is a little more restrictive; you're permitted to have only four hens there. Again, no roosters.

In rural areas outside any municipality's city limits, you can own up to 99 hens before you have to register them with the province.

A FINAL WORD ABOUT OUR ANIMAL FRIENDS

Animal Protection

One of British Columbia's first animal protection statutes was a Vancouver bylaw that was adopted in 1892. Specifically, the provision prohibited anyone from "ill-using or mal-treating [sic] any animal or animals in any manner whatsoever whether by negligently ommitting [sic] properly to feed the same, beating, overdriving or useing [sic] the same when infirm, lame or suffering, or by overloading the same."

Can't say much for the Founding Fathers' spelling and punctuation, but they did subject violators to a $100 fine (over $2300 today) and up to two months in jail.

That Will Teach Fido

There were a lot of unprovoked attacks by otherwise docile pets and farm animals in the 1870s. So, in 1875, the BC Legislative Assembly enacted a law allowing a person to sue "for injuries caused by animals of a domestic nature" without having to allege or prove that the animal's owner "knew, or had the means of knowledge, that the animal was or is of a vicious or mischievous nature, or was or is accustomed to [doing] acts causing injury."

Beware of German Sheep Dogs

A 1936 Township of Langley bylaw required every dog owner to get a licence. The licence fee was $1 per year for a male dog and $2 for a female. There were two exceptions. First, the fee for a "German Sheep Dog" (aka the famous German shepherd or Alsatian) was $5, regardless of sex. Second, anyone with five or more dogs was charged a flat $10 per year.

No Pets!

A 1964 Coquitlam bylaw prohibited live animals and birds from being kept in any room in a restaurant or other commercial establishment where food or drink was prepared, stored, served or sold. Makes sense, but what's interesting is that the city fathers felt the need to specifically forbid cats, dogs, canaries, parrots and parakeets in the bylaw. Apparently somebody was bringing their pets to work.

Hush, Polly

An Oak Bay bylaw requires the community's residents to keep their noisy parrots quiet. Polly can no longer squawk when she wants a cracker.

Food

*If it's true that you are what you eat, thank goodness
there are bylaws to make sure you get what you pay for.*

BREAD...

How Big Is that Loaf?

The Vancouver City Council in 1887 passed a bylaw requiring all loaves of bread sold or sitting on the shelf at a bakery to weigh 1.5 pounds (675 grams). To allow for shrinkage, one 24-hour-old loaf of bread of lesser weight was allowed for every fresh loaf that met the requirements. And the chief of police was to visit every bakery in the city at least once every 60 days to weigh the loaves and confiscate any that weren't up to snuff.

The bylaw was changed five years later to exempt biscuits, buns, rolls, crackers, muffins and other "fancy cakes" from its provisions. (Can you imagine a 1.5-pound [675-gram] roll?) But the names of all bakers who sold or stocked lightweight bread were now to be published in the local daily newspaper, and anyone who violated the law faced a $100 fine (over $2300 today) and up to two months in jail.

The bylaw was changed again in 1899 so that fresh "fancy bread" had to weigh only 1.25 pounds (560 grams). Fancy breads included whole wheat, rye and French rolls. And loaves of fancy bread could weigh less if they were more than 18 hours old.

What's in that Loaf?

In 1909, a new Vancouver bylaw made it illegal for professional bakers to make or sell any bread containing "deletorius [sic] materials" such as borax, sulphate of copper, sulphate of zinc, chalk or carbonate of magnesia. It was also unlawful to sell bread that consisted of more than three percent ash. Kind of makes one wonder what the bakers were putting into their bread!

...AND BUTTER

Well, Margarine...

That substitute for butter we are all so familiar with had a tough time getting a foothold in British Columbia.

A federal law in place for most of the period between 1886 and 1948 banned the sale of margarine in Canada. (The prohibition was lifted from 1917 to 1923 because of dairy shortages caused by World War I.)

The Canadian Supreme Court gave the ban the boot in 1948. Afraid that consumers might confuse margarine with butter, and fearing the collapse of the local butter industry, the BC Legislative Assembly passed the Oleomargarine Act in 1949.

The law stated that "no oleomargarine shall have a tint or shade containing more than one and six-tenths of yellow, or of yellow and red collectively, measured in terms of the

Lovibond tintometer scale." (In other words, while butter may be yellow, margarine must be white.)

A special licence from the provincial government was also needed to make margarine or to sell it wholesale. Restaurants and other public eating places were not allowed to mix margarine with butter. Finally, all public places that used margarine had to prominently display on their menus, or have a conspicuous sign in every room where food was served, a statement that said, "Oleomargarine is served here as a substitute for butter."

British Columbia became the first province in Canada to legalize yellow margarine in 1952. However, the "Oleo is served here" notice requirements remained on the books for years.

Booze

Alcohol flowed freely in British Columbia's early days; it was even once the sole source of revenue for the government's coffers. But then the pendulum swung the other direction and drink was banned. The status quo is now somewhere in the middle, but only after some absurd laws about the consumption of booze were enacted.

ALCOHOL BEFORE PROHIBITION

Early Days...

Drinking was a very popular activity in British Columbia during the 19th century. Yale had 13 saloons all within 50 metres of each other at the height of the Fraser Canyon Gold Rush. Victoria had 149 licensed saloons in 1864 (at a time when the city had only five police officers) and New Westminster had one licensed bar for every 13 residents in 1880. There were over 45 saloons conducting business on Vancouver's Waterfront alone in 1888, and the examples go on and on. Indeed, you could buy a drink in over 1000 locations across BC by 1900. And all of them were allowed to remain open 24/7 until 1891.

Great Source of Tax Revenue

Want to live in a place where there's no income, sales or property taxes? Well, get into your time machine and go back to Vancouver Island in the 1850s. During most of that decade, the fees charged by the colony for commercial liquor licences (£100 for a wholesale licence and £125 for a retail one, or about $12,600 and $15,800 today) constituted 100 percent of the colonial government's income!

No Native Drinking
The very first laws enacted in both the Colony of Vancouver Island and the mainland Colony of British Columbia dealt with the sale of alcohol to members of the First Nations. It was banned.

Governor Richard Blanshard of Vancouver Island issued his proclamation on May 13, 1850, and Governor James Douglas of BC read his on September 6, 1858. Native liquor laws continued after the colonies merged in 1866 and joined Confederation five years later, and it remained illegal to sell alcohol to any member of the First Nations in BC until 1962. In contrast, the prohibition against selling liquor to non-Natives in British Columbia lasted only from 1917 to 1921.

Wait Until You're 16 Before You Try That!
A lot of ships in the 1860s, from canoes to steamers, delivered liquor to whomever they pleased along the British Columbia coastline while others sailed through BC's waters to sell it to Natives in Alaska.

The Indian Liquor Ordinance of 1867 is possibly the first BC statute to apply to criminal acts committed outside the province's borders. Specifically:

> *Any person selling, bartering, or giving, or attempting to sell, barter, or give intoxicating liquor to any Indian of*

the Continent of North America, or of the Islands
adjacent thereto, shall be liable on conviction for each
offense, to a fine not exceeding five hundred dollars.

That $500 would be worth about $7580 today. Also, a second conviction under the law could land a person in jail for up to 12 months.

And whether it was their first offence or not, if the defendant was under the age of 16, the judge "may order such offender to be once or twice privately whipped" in lieu of the fine or imprisonment.

CASE FILE
Half Rations in the Dark

The punishment for being drunk and disorderly in Victoria in the late 19th century could be quite harsh. The following passage was recorded in a Victoria City Police charge book: "March 25, 1876, Jennie an Indian woman charged with drunk and disorderly. Sentence 14 days in gaol [i.e., jail] on half food rations and to be confined in a dark cell every second day."

Servant v. Apprentice

One of the first bylaws that Vancouver ever adopted was the 1886 prohibition against giving an intoxicating drink to any apprentice or servant without the prior consent of their "master." The servant's union must have been active in those days because the reference to servants was deleted six years later. The prohibition against serving a drink to an apprentice, however, continued for many years after that.

Be Careful Who You Trust

Under the Indian Liquor Ordinance of 1867, informers were entitled, at the discretion of the judge, to one-third of the fines collected.

Nor to a Drunkard

The Liquor License Regulation Act of 1891 allowed the province's local courts to designate a person as a "drunkard" if the individual "by excessive drinking of liquor, misspends, wastes, or lessens his estate, or greatly injures his health, or endangers or interrupts the peace and happiness of his family."

To be declared a "drunkard" meant that no one in BC, except a doctor or a minister, could legally sell or give you any alcohol for one year. Anyone who gave you a drink faced a fine of up to $50, or $100 for second and subsequent violations. The statute even allowed for you to appear before a judge to have the act applied against yourself.

No More Gambling at Saloons

A lot of cowboy movies show gambling in bars and saloons. Those days ended in British Columbia in 1899 when "draw poker, stud poker, black jack, faro, or any other games of chance to be played for money...or other devices that represent money" were banned from all places that had a retail liquor licence.

Accommodations Required

For those areas of BC outside the limits of an incorporated city, district, town or village, the Liquor Licence Act of 1900 required all hotels, inns, beer houses and "other places of public entertainment" seeking a liquor licence to have at least four bedrooms "with sufficient complement of bedding and furniture to accommodate the traveling [sic] public." The law also required these establishments to have an attached stable large enough for at least six horses plus "appliances for keeping a well-appointed eating house for serving meals to travelers [sic]."

No Water!

A 1907 Vancouver bylaw made it illegal for a theatre to have "any so called green room, or any room or rooms, such as may be used for sitting rooms for actors, or persons frequenting such show or exhibition, in which liquor, wine, beer, or other beverage, *whether intoxicating or not*, is sold or given away." (Emphasis added.)

So much for a simple glass of water during intermission.

Happily Married Women Need Not Apply

Starting in 1910, liquor licences could be granted to only certain types of individuals.

Licences could be given to men provided they were adults, had lived in BC for 12 months and were registered voters.

The latter requirement meant that no licences could be issued to Canadians of Asian or First Nations descent.

Liquor licences could also be issued to adult spinsters and widows, but a married woman could get one only if she was living separate and apart from her spouse and if her husband did not "lodge or live in, upon, or about" the hotel.

Furthermore, an unmarried or widowed woman holding a liquor licence automatically lost it to her husband if she got married. If hubby was not legally qualified to hold the licence, the Superintendent of the Provincial Police had the power to cancel it or give it to someone else.

No Booze for You

The 1910 amendments to the Liquor Licence Act made it illegal to sell alcohol (retail or wholesale) or otherwise give any booze to the following individuals:

☞ Alcoholics (the statute referred to them as "dipsomaniacs")

☞ People who were "openly and notoriously addicted to drunken debauches or sprees" (a rather nebulous category of people)

☞ People who "openly and notoriously" wasted their money in drinking liquor and riotous living (another vague classification)

☞ "Vagrants and tramps" (the latter was then a gender-neutral term referring to vagrants who travelled from place to place)

☞ Taxi drivers (the law called them "chauffeurs operating any vehicle propelled by power...for the carriage of passengers for hire," so horse-drawn carriage drivers could still indulge)

☞ Prostitutes (no guidance was given as to how to spot one)

☞ And, of course, minors and members of the First Nations

The CPR's Dry Belt Zone

In 1870, to facilitate the construction of the Canadian Pacific Railway across western Canada, Parliament enacted the Act for the Preservation of Peace on Public Works. Among other things, the law established a 20-mile (32-kilometre) wide belt (10 miles [16 kilometres] on both sides of the railroad's surveyed line) where the sale of alcohol was illegal. Violators were subject to a $40 fine (about $670 today) on their first and second offence and possible six months imprisonment on their third.

Enforcement was left to the North-West Mounted Police, but their job was a difficult one, in no small part thanks to the BC government. As to those parts of the railroad construction that were within BC, the provincial government complained that the law improperly denied British Columbia the revenue it would have otherwise received from the sale of liquor licences, and it freely issued licences to anyone who wanted to sell alcohol within the dry belt despite the federal law.

Drunkenness brought railroad construction to a virtual halt. Eventually, the Mounties' Sam Steele convinced the federal government in 1884 to enlarge the no-alcohol zone to 20 miles on either side of the railroad and to make the second offence punishable by jail time. That did the trick. Liquor-selling establishments strung along the edge of the dry belt now had to move, and the navvies who were once willing to walk 10 miles for a drink found 20 too far to go.

What a Guy Will Do to Get a Drink

All sorts of ways were invented to bring alcohol into the CPR dry belt: metal kegs full of liquor were hidden in barrels of kerosene; mincemeats and peaches were soaked in brandy; and tin containers that looked like Bibles contained booze inside. Eggs were even emptied of their yolks and filled with alcohol.

PROHIBITION AND BEYOND

Don't Trust a Drinking Soldier's Vote

The citizens of British Columbia approved prohibition in a 1916 referendum. The initial results were overwhelming: 36,392 to 27,217. Only Alberni, Fernie and Lillooet voted against it. But when the ballots cast by BC soldiers fighting World War I in Europe were added, it was discovered that Prohibition actually failed by 822 votes! Irregularities in the soldiers' vote were soon discovered, including evidence that free beer had been used to influence their decision, and most of their ballots were cast aside. Prohibition came into effect in BC in 1917.

Booze As Medicine

The British Columbia Prohibition Act banned the sale of alcohol except for sacramental, medicinal and industrial purposes. However, doctors, druggists, dentists and veterinarians (and their patients, if they had a written prescription) could purchase liquor from government-appointed vendors.

It was already very common to use liquor as medicine. Now, with the sale of booze illegal, many physicians were charging $2 (that's about $25 today) for diagnoses that called for alcohol as a remedy. There were 181,350 such prescriptions in Vancouver alone in 1919. One physician even wrote 4100 prescriptions for liquor in one month! And as noted by one government official, "in Vancouver queues a quarter of a mile [400 metres] long could be seen waiting their turn to enter the liquor stores to get prescriptions filled."

Hey, Doc, Want Some Second-hand Liquor?

The enforcement of the Prohibition Act was left to the municipalities, and the province provided no financial help. It cost Vancouver alone $100,000 per year to enforce the statute.

However, all seized liquor had to be turned over to the provincial government, which, in turn, sold it at a profit to doctors, druggists, dentists, veterinarians, clergymen, manufacturers and anyone with a medical prescription.

Drink Only at Home

Although the sale of alcohol was banned, British Columbians could still make, possess and drink liquor, but only at their own "dwelling house." That meant, under the law, a location actually and exclusively occupied and used as a private residence. Sorry, but no drinking was allowed in your hotel room. Cabins (even those with stoves and beds) as well as trailers, bunkhouses, float houses, tents and boats, all of which were used by many British Columbians at the time as their primary place of residence, were not considered "dwelling houses." Apartments were, but only as long as a whole series of rules were met.

And it had to be *your* house or apartment! The possession or drinking of alcohol anywhere else, even your friend's place of residence, put you afoul of the law with the potential for a fine of between $50 and $100 ($830 to $1660 in today's dollars) or 35 to 60 days in jail. And don't give your houseguests any drinks. The first offence would bring you a mandatory 6- to 12-month prison sentence with no option of a fine!

Necessity is the Mother of…Near Beer and Beerless

The Prohibition Act defined liquor as any beverage that was more than 2.5 percent proof (1.25 percent alcohol), allowing local breweries to produce "near beer," which was 2.5 percent proof, and "beerless" that was only 2 percent proof. As can be imagined, both near beer and beerless became rather popular drinks in the province.

Other "beverages" that became fashionable during Prohibition were vanilla-, orange-, lemon- and other flavoured extracts that were 2 percent proof; they were so popular that it was once proposed their sale should be made illegal, too.

Turning "Innocent Until Proven Guilty" on Its Head

The Prohibition Act brought three radical changes to BC's criminal system.

First, police could enter any building (including a person's home) or vehicle without a warrant if they believed that liquor was being unlawfully kept or sold there.

Second, the mere presence of illegal alcohol on your premises could create a presumption in court that you were guilty of unlawfully selling liquor, even if someone else (for example, your kid or an employee) had brought the booze to your place without your knowledge.

Finally, once charged of an offence under the act, a defendant had to prove his innocence rather than the Crown prove his guilt.

The Death of Prohibition

British Columbians voted to abandon Prohibition by almost two to one in a referendum in October 1920. However, the plebiscite did not bring back the bars and saloons that existed before 1917; in fact, that wasn't even an option. Because of the extreme volatility of the issue, the voters only got to choose between Prohibition and the strict government control of the liquor industry. They choose the latter. Prohibition officially ended in 1921.

We're Number One

British Columbia was the first jurisdiction in English-speaking North America to repeal Prohibition. Québec beat BC by a few months.

No Fun in Booze

BC's Government Liquor Act of 1921 and the regulations adopted under it by the newly established Liquor Control Board (LCB) took most of the fun out of the drinking. These regulations included the following:

☛ You could buy alcohol only at a government retail liquor store

☛ The government liquor stores could not be open longer than eight hours a day or after 8:00 PM

☛ You needed a government permit to buy alcohol. The permit cost $5 per year (which was nearly a day's wages for the average worker in 1921) and was issued only after you passed a character check. You had to show the permit and have it stamped each time you bought a bottle at a government liquor store.

☛ The drinking of any alcoholic beverage in public, including beer, was illegal. This ban included restaurants and public lounges as well as outdoor venues such as baseball games and family picnics at a park.

☛ The private sale of near beer was outlawed

Get Thee Home

To encourage beer drinkers to go home after work and stay there, the LCB required in November 1942 that all beer parlours be closed from 6:00 PM to 7:00 PM. A few months later, the LCB further decreed that the parlours could only be open from 2:00 PM to 6:00 PM and from 7:00 PM to 11:00 PM.

Don't Want to Shop There

The first retail liquor store operated by the LCB opened on
June 15, 1921. LCB regulations, however, made sure that
these stores were not very welcoming places.

- ☛ Prices were set by the government and were high. You could
  no longer get a five-cent glass of beer but had to buy it by the
  bottle or, for $3.50 (more than $40 today), by the case.

- ☛ A store could only be identified by one small outdoor sign that
  said "Open."

- ☛ Any public display that contained the words "bar," "bar-room,"
  "saloon" or "tavern" was illegal.

- ☛ Curtains had to be drawn or windows blocked so no one could
  look inside.

- ☛ Customers were not allowed to handle any bottles until they
  had filled out written orders and paid in cash.

- ☛ The stores had the authority to limit how much anyone could
  buy.

Get Around the Law

One of the goals behind the Government Liquor Act was
to prevent people from getting together to drink socially.
Between 1921 and 1925, one common way to get around this
was to establish private "clubs" at former saloons, with mem-
bership fees as low as 10 cents, where the "members" drank
liquor that they brought with them. Veterans' clubs also
circumvented the law by admitting only their members and
selling them tickets for beer so that no money was exchanged
across the bar.

Regs at Beer Parlours

Just like the government liquor retail stores, BC's beer parlours faced a number of legal restrictions:

- ☞ As with the stores, only a small sign that said "Open" was allowed; anything that proclaimed "bar" or "tavern" was illegal, and it wasn't until 1933 that parlours could even brag that they had a licence.

- ☞ Beer was the only beverage allowed until the 1950s (and, even then, it was only beer and wine).

- ☞ Women were not allowed to work in a beer parlour unless they owned it.

- ☞ Customers could not go to the counter or service bar; instead, a waiter had to take their orders and serve the beer at their table.

- ☞ Customers had to be seated while they drank. No standing allowed.

- ☞ It was illegal to sell food, soft drinks or cigarettes in a beer parlour, and all forms of entertainment, including games, dancing and music, were forbidden. Patrons weren't even allowed to play checkers or sing! (So much for karaoke.)

No Women Here!

Beer parlour owners feared in the 1920s that those who wanted to bring back Prohibition would equate the presence of women in the parlours with prostitution and make a big deal about it. To avoid that, the British Columbia Hotel Association banned all female customers from beer parlours in 1926. (All parlours were located in hotels.) The ban was voluntary and it applied only to Vancouver—and it only lasted nine months before people started to ignore it.

Partition

In 1942, the LCB ordered all beer parlours in Vancouver, Prince Rupert and Esquimalt to erect barriers to physically separate male patrons from the "ladies and their [male] escorts." Parlours elsewhere in the province were strongly encouraged to do the same. The move, in essence, turned every beer parlour in British Columbia into two.

The partitions had to be at least 6 feet (1.8 metres) high (later increased to 6 feet, 9 inches [2 metres]) and allow "no visibility" between the two sections. One 8-foot-wide opening (2.5 metres) was permitted for the comings and goings of the waiters, but customers were not allowed to pass through it.

The men-only and the mixed sections had to have their own street entrances. Men's toilets had to be installed on both the ladies' side (for the escorts, of course) and the men's side. To go from one section of the parlour to visit the washroom and then head to the other section on your way out was forbidden. Each section also had to have its own pay telephone.

Because one service bar usually supplied the drinks for both the male-only and mixed sections, the LCB sometimes mandated that particular parlours have, between the partition and the bar, locked gates or gates that could be opened only by an electric device. The board even required some parlours to post guards at those gates and at the parlours' street entrances.

No Crossing!

Once the LCB required partitions, it became illegal for people to cross over from the men-only side to the mixed side, and vice-a-versa, as well as for men to wander from table to table on the mixed side.

I'm Being Cheated!

Beer parlours were prohibited by the LCB to raise their prices, so two things happened when the federal and provincial governments increased their taxes on beer during World War II.

First, the parlours started to sell beer in smaller glasses. The LCB did not require a specific glass size, and most beer was previously sold in 8-ounce (240-millilitre) glasses. Now they were sold in 7.25-ounce (215-millilitre) glasses.

Second, some parlours started to pour less beer and more foam.

Both actions led to a flood of complaints to the government. In response, a new LCB regulation in 1945 limited the froth on beer glasses to half an inch (1.25 centimetres). One year later, all BC beer parlours had to use glasses that had a clearly marked fill or load line, known as a "Plimsoll Line," which guaranteed that the glass contained at least 6.5 ounces (190 millilitres) of beer (still leaving almost 20 percent of the glass filled with foam).

CASE FILE
No Liquor for Her

It was illegal from 1854 to 1962 under BC law to sell liquor to any member of the First Nations.

A woman was denied a drink at Vancouver's Regent Hotel in 1948 for the reason that she looked like a Native. She wasn't. Her friend complained to the LCB, which replied, "Mrs. K. is partly of the Indian Race and her facial characteristics are such as to place a waiter in a beer parlour on his guard." The LCB's suggested solution? That Mrs. K. obtain and carry with her an official letter "to the effect that she is not deemed to be an Indian within the meaning of the [federal] Indian Act."

No Mixed Couples

Because the LCB had the authority to suspend or cancel
any licence "for any such reason as the Board may seem
sufficient," there were a whole series of unwritten rules that
the LCB was able to enforce. For example, the LCB "encouraged" beer parlours not to serve black men or mixed-raced
couples. But while a couple consisting of a white woman
and a man of any other ethnic group was considered "mixed,"
a white man with a woman of different ethnicity was not.

No Ladies and Gentlemen
The LCB ordered in 1953 all beer parlours to label their
washroom doors simply as "Men" and "Women." Other
words such as "Gents" and "Ladies" were strictly prohibited.
According to the LCB, such alternatives were "flippant" and
diminished "the dignity that should surround the privilege
of [having a liquor] licence." Furthermore, the rule would
stay in effect "until we are sure that the patrons are all ladies
and gentlemen."

Can't Say "Tap"

A group of entrepreneurs wanted to open a restaurant in
Vancouver in 1998 called The Newfie Tap and Grill.
However, BC's liquor laws prohibit the use of the word "tap"
in a restaurant's name. So the Newfie Tap and Grill became
the Atlantic Trap and Gill!

More Recent Innovations
Licensed restaurants could again serve alcoholic drinks without meals or with only an appetizer-sized food order starting
in 1999. That was the same year that shoppers were first permitted to use their credit cards to buy liquor at retail outlets.

Too Much Beer

The LCB limit in 1953 was two glasses of beer per customer; any more than that and the beer parlour and the waiter could be criminally charged.

Doggie Bag It

It was not until 2002 that restaurant patrons could start taking home their unfinished bottles of wine.

No Entertainment Here!
It was illegal until 1954 for a pub to have live music, a television or even a radio. It wasn't until 1999 that restrictions on the number of TV sets, and even their screen size, were removed.

Inheritance

Among the English laws that British Columbia acquired when Vancouver Island and the BC mainland became colonies were those governing the distribution of a person's estate when the decedent died without a will.

The majority of adult British Columbians who died in the late 19th century either had a will or, more likely, owned so little property that their estates did not have to be probated when they died. However, 38 percent of British Columbians who passed away had been rich enough that their land and other possessions had to be distributed by the courts but were careless and hadn't left any written instructions as to where their property should go upon their death.

PASSING IT ON

A Wife's Personal Property

The law regarding the succession of personal property that was brought to BC from Britain was the nearly 200-year-old Statute of Distribution (adopted by England in 1670 with minor changes in 1677 and 1685).

Under that act, all of a wife's personal property (money, clothes, jewellery and other belongings) became her husband's upon her death regardless of any surviving children or other relatives. Only if hubby was already dead would her kids or anyone from her side of the family get anything.

...And Her Husband's

In contrast, a widow in BC inherited only one-third of her husband's personal property, with their children equally dividing the remaining two-thirds. If the couple had no kids, the wife got one-half of the property and the husband's next of kin got the other. If a man died and left behind children but no surviving wife, the kids equally shared everything. And if there were neither widow nor kiddies, the man's next of kin got it all.

Who Writes These Rules?

Who was the next of kin of a deceased husband depended on a set of rules. For starters, if hubby's father was still alive, he was the sole next of kin. If his dad was already dead, then the decedent's mom and his siblings all equally shared as next of kin. Likewise, if both of the husband's parents were dead, then his personal property would be divided equally between his siblings. If there were no brothers or sisters left, then their children (the decedent's nephews and nieces) would be the next of kin, followed by the husband's grandparents, uncles and aunts, first cousins and so on (in that order). At no time would any of the wife's relatives get any part of the husband's personal estate, even if it included that green dress or diamond necklace he inherited from his spouse.

What's Good for the Goose...

There used to be two legal concepts in the English common law regarding the succession of real estate known as "dower" and "curtesy." Both were part of the law that British Columbia inherited from England in the mid-19th century.

Dower is centuries old. It entitled a wife to use for the rest of her life (i.e., a "life estate") one-third of all the land that her deceased husband owned when they were wed or that he purchased during their marriage. However, a husband could sell his land, give it away or dispose of it in a will without his wife's consent.

Curtesy essentially worked the same way, except that it gave the husband a life estate in all (not just one-third) of his wife's land. But there was also another odd little difference between dower and curtesy. Dower was not dependent upon whether the couple had any kids, but the husband had no rights under curtesy unless a child had been born alive to the couple during their marriage. (It did not matter if the child was still alive at the time of the wife's death.)

Old, Crazy Rules

Now, if you think the rules regarding the inheritance of personal property were strange, try those dealing with the distribution of real property when the decedent had no will.

The statute that British Columbia inherited from England was the Inheritance Act of 1833, which codified a whole series of legal principles collectively known as primogeniture that date back to the feudal 13th century. As a result, in almost every instance, only one person (a man) would inherit all of the decedent's real property.

First, subject to the rights of the surviving spouse under dower and curtesy, all the intestate's real property went to the eldest son, leaving the rest of the kids with nothing. Second, if the eldest was already dead, his eldest son got it all, and if that kid was deceased, then *his* eldest son inherited, and so on. This meant that the second son of the original decedent would get the property only if all of his older brother's lineal descendants had already met their maker. Finally, the intestate's daughters got nothing at all unless all their brothers and their lineal descendants had predeceased the girls' father—and even then they'd all have to equally share in their dad's estate.

Are These Rules Any Better?

How real property was distributed in BC changed with the adoption of the Inheritance Act of 1872. According to that statute, whenever a married person died without a will, the surviving spouse only received the life estate that was coming to them under dower and curtesy. That individual did not own the property, could not sell or otherwise dispose of it, nor encumber it with any debts or obligations. Since, under BC law at the time, everything a wife acquired both during before and during her marriage was her husband's property, this really did not affect the men too much. However, limiting the wife to the life estate that she was already entitled to under dower meant that there was very little she could do with any real estate that her spouse left behind.

The first in line to inherit real property (to unconditionally do with as they wished) was the decedent's lineal descendants. In other words, the dead person's children (both male and female) would divide the property equally among themselves.

However, if the decedent had no lineal descendants, then his dad inherited everything! It didn't matter if the dead guy's wife or mother were still alive or if he had brothers and sisters; father got it all. The only exception was if the dearly departed got the property from his mother or from her side of the family to begin with, in which case his mom inherited the land.

I'll Disinherit Her!

For over half a century, a mean-spirited man in British Columbia could leave his spouse and kids nothing at all simply by writing a will. This changed, however, when the BC Legislative Assembly adopted the Testator's Family Maintenance Act in 1920. That statute allowed a surviving wife and children to seek a court order to ignore the will and make "adequate provision for the proper maintenance and support" of the testator's surviving family. However, there was no guarantee that the order would be granted, and a judge could deny support if he didn't approve of the widow's character or conduct. Even if the order was granted, there were no guidelines as to how much support the family would receive; rather, it was whatever the judge thought "adequate, just and equitable under the circumstances."

Throw in Some Sex

With adoption of the Land Registry Act of 1925, a spouse's right to inherit was based for the first time on that person's sexual conduct! For example, if a man had left his wife and was living "in sin" at the time of his wife's passing, or had committed adultery anytime before her death, then he could not inherit one dime if she died without a will. Likewise, if he had left his wife without cause two or more years before her death, he also could not inherit anything.

Family

There are few things that are more important to people, and harder to change as attitudes and behaviours evolve, than laws governing family relationships. Want to get married? Want to dip into the family assets? Want to know who gets the kids when there's a divorce? The whats and wherefores are all laid out in the law. And while they may have made sense to British Columbians in the province's early days, some of the original rules and regulations would be considered downright crazy today.

THE INS AND OUTS OF MARRIAGE

I Want to Get Married!

An 1867 BC law provided three ways for a couple to get hitched.

First, they could go the traditional route—get a marriage licence, and have a religious wedding. Under the statute, all "ministers and clergymen of every church and religious denomination in British Columbia" could perform weddings, and the licence cost $5, or about $75 in today's money.

Not enough money for a licence? No problem. The bride and groom could still have a religious wedding. The second way to get married was have the minister or priest publicize the banns of marriage openly in an audible voice (so everyone could hear) in any church, chapel or place of public worship that the couple were connected with for three consecutive Sundays "during divine service." If that was done, the man and woman were husband and wife.

(The 1867 law also provided for the marriage of Jews and Quakers according to the "rites and ceremonies" of their own faith.)

But what if the bride and groom wanted a civil wedding? The third way to get married was for the couple to file a written notice of their intent to marry with their local government registrar. After waiting at least 14 days (during which time their notice would be kept in a book that was open for all to see), the couple could get married at the registrar's office, but only between 10:00 AM and 4:00 PM. Registrars were also entitled to charge $10 for their time.

You Can't Get Married in Secret

The 1867 law required that, unless a couple's marriage licence said otherwise, all weddings had to be done "in a public manner" with the doors of the church or registrar's office kept open. (Perhaps to allow the bride or groom a quick exit in case they changed their minds?) And the wedding had to be performed in the presence of at least two "credible" witnesses.

I Object!

A certificate of marriage was promptly issued to a couple once they were married. However, anyone could, after paying $2.50, file a "caveat" with the local registrar to prevent the certificate from being issued. Everything was then put on hold until the registrar looked into whether any reason might exist not to grant the certificate. (For example, the bride or groom might be underage.) If one was found, the marriage was void.

Dad Has Last Say

Under the 1867 law, you had to be at least 21 to get married. However, you could get hitched at a younger age if you had your father's consent. If dad was dead, then you needed your guardian's approval. The guardian, of course, was usually appointed by your father in his will or by the court, and the person chosen was not necessarily mom. Only if dad was dead and there was no guardian could you go to your mother to get permission, and even then only if she was unmarried. Sorry, but if mom had remarried, whether or not she consented to your nuptials was irrelevant; you were out of luck.

If dad, mom or the guardian were mentally incompetent or many kilometres away (the words used in the statute were "*non compos mentis*, or in parts beyond the seas"), or they were unreasonably denying their permission or were doing so for "undue motives," then you could go to court to get permission.

By the way, the age requirement did not apply to a widow or widower. But what if you were under 21 and merely divorced? Sorry again. You still needed dad's approval to marry.

Too Young to Marry

Just how young could you marry if dad consented? The 1867 statute did not specify a minimum age. However, one of the British laws that was still in force in BC (and would be well into the 20th century) was that a girl as young as 12 and a boy of 14 could wed as long as they had their father's approval. In fact, as long as the bride or groom was seven or older, a marriage of sorts could go ahead. Such a marriage was considered "imperfect" or voidable, meaning that the wedding would become valid as soon as the bride and groom turned 12 and 14 respectively, as long as they didn't do anything on their 12th or 14th birthday to repudiate their vows. A marriage of someone under the age of seven was invalid no matter what.

WIFELY RIGHTS
Everything She Owns Is Mine!

The English law inherited by BC in the mid-19th century gave a married man near-total control of his family's property. Furthermore, most of these provisions were not altered or repealed in BC until well into the 20th century.

Once she said "I do," all of a woman's personal belongings, including her wages and everything she bought, inherited or otherwise acquired before or during marriage, became her spouse's property that he could use or dispose of as he wished. A wife kept legal ownership of her land, but her husband had exclusive control of it (including the ability to sell it), as well as total control over rents or other income that the property might produce, as long as they were married.

A married woman also had no rights to any jointly accumulated family assets. Her husband was entitled to her unpaid labour (i.e., he could force her to work at his business), and any income or property obtained belonged solely to him. He could even give away all of his family's property in his will.

Your Credit Isn't Good Here

At a time when a divorce was almost impossible to get, the English common law (and, hence, BC law) gave an abandoned wife the right to purchase necessities on her husband's credit, but few businesses were willing to extend credit on the account of a man who was no longer around. And if a man should desert his spouse and later return, he and his creditors could seize any property that she acquired during his absence since, after all, it legally belonged to him. A married woman also could not sign a contract nor start a lawsuit on her own behalf.

You Can Get Help, But Only if You're a Good Girl

Victoria's economy during the early 1860s was dependent in large part to the ups and downs faced by the miners in the Fraser River and Cariboo gold rushes. If a claim went south, or if the supplies and equipment that the miners purchased on credit from merchants and manufacturers were lost or damaged on the way to the gold fields, both the miners and their creditors in Victoria went broke. Because debtors were often imprisoned, many men simply fled to avoid jail, leaving behind in Victoria abandoned wives and children who had to fend for themselves with no legal ability to enter into contracts (e.g., an employment contract or even a simple purchase of groceries) or to own property (like the clothes on their back).

In response to this situation, the Colony of Vancouver Island adopted the Deserted Wives Act in 1862. The law allowed a married woman to go to court and obtain a protection order that gave her the right to own property, sign contracts or sue as if she were a single woman. The order also protected her property from her husband's and his creditors' claims. No waiting period was required, and a husband or creditor who wrongfully seized a wife's protected property could be sued.

The statute, however, did have severe limitations. First, as its name implied, its provisions were available only to deserted wives; women who continued to live with their husbands or who had left their spouse, no matter how abusive, drunk or irresponsible he was, were out of luck. Furthermore, before a protection order could be granted, a judge had to be satisfied that the woman had been deserted "without reasonable cause." Self-assertive, insubordinate and uppity wives need not apply.

Second, the law also required the woman to be chaste, of moral character and earning a respectable living "by her own industry or property," which meant no boyfriends, no illegal occupations and no dependence on charity. The orders also applied only to the property the wife acquired after the order was issued; husbands could still get their hands on and dispose of anything she got during the interim, no matter how long it had been since he had deserted her. (Records indicate that most women applying for a protection did so only after their property was in jeopardy and, by then, it was too late.) Finally, the law allowed husbands and their creditors to go to a judge and petition to have the protection order rescinded.

Money for the Wife and Kiddies

The Deserted Wives' Maintenance Act of 1901 finally allowed a woman to go to court to seek a support order against her deadbeat husband if he was "able wholly or in part to maintain" her and their kids but had "willfully refused or neglected" to do so. The definition of "desertion" was rather broad; it included a wife that had been abandoned, as well as one that had left her spouse either because of assault or other acts of cruelty or because of his "refusal or neglect, without sufficient cause, to supply her with food and other necessaries of life when able to do so."

A judge could grant up to $20 a week (or about $510 a week in today's money); if the husband refused to pay, his personal property could be seized (if there was any within the court's jurisdiction—and there usually wasn't) and sold at auction.

Sounds pretty good, right? Well, there was a catch; the law basically gave control of the wife's sex life to the man who deserted her. The missus and the kids were entitled to no support at all if it was proven that she'd ever had sex with a man other than her husband, even if it occurred before her marriage (or, for that matter, even before she met hubby), unless her husband "condoned" the act. Likewise, any support order granted by the court could be withdrawn at the judge's discretion if the wife was caught fooling around after the order had been given. In contrast, hubby's bedroom activities were entirely irrelevant to the support proceedings.

Reform?

A new Deserted Wives' Maintenance Act was adopted in 1911. The maximum a wife could get was still $20 a week, but now the husband's wages and bank accounts could be garnished and he could end up in jail for up to 30 days if he didn't pay. Although the ban against the wife committing adultery before the support order was granted was still in place, she was now free to do whatever she wanted after the order was approved.

However, for every two steps forward, there is often one step back. Women who owned property in their own right that was "sufficient for the comfortable maintenance of herself and of the infant children (if any)" could no longer get a support order against their husbands. The financial support of a couple's children was now, once again, primarily mom's responsibility.

Be Careful Lending Her Money

During the 1860s and early 1870s, despite their inability under BC law to own property and sign contracts, more and more married women in BC were going into business, negotiating deals and getting credit from merchants, manufacturers and bankers. However, anyone dealing with these women did so at their own risk, as two Victoria businessmen could attest. Both men had loaned money to married women, but when they tried to collect, the courts ruled against them. After all, a wife could not legally enter a contract and, thus, she was not bound by what she had signed.

Be Careful Lending to Him, Too

The Married Women's Property Act of 1873 protected a wife's property from her husband's creditors, but it also allowed her spouse to transfer to her unlimited amounts of his own real property so he could avoid his creditors (which was seen as a good thing by many, given the severe economic recession that BC was going through at the time).

CASE FILE
What's a Girl to Do?
(Or, A Tale of One Province and Two Laws)

The Deserted Wives Act was one of the few laws that remained in effect on Vancouver Island, but only on the island, after the colony merged with the mainland in 1866. Had the statute applied to all of British Columbia, Lytton resident Maria Cheffrey would have been out of luck.

Mrs. Cheffrey travelled to Victoria in 1872 to get a protection order under the act. She and her husband were married in 1866 but separated after four months. Mr. Cheffrey went off to live in the Peace River area while his wife successfully supported herself during the following six years. She even acquired real estate in both Lytton and Victoria, but then her husband returned.

Matthew Begbie was the judge who heard Maria's case. He knew that the Deserted Wives Act enabled him to protect only the property and earnings that Mrs. Cheffrey had obtained *after* the date of any order that he granted. Therefore, everything Maria acquired since her husband left in 1866 still legally belonged to him, and she would lose it all. Fortunately, Begbie noticed that the two parties lived on the mainland.

The Colony of British Columbia, when it was established in 1858, inherited British law as it existed that year, not as it had existed in 1849 when the Colony of Vancouver Island was created. Luckily for Mrs. Cheffrey, the British Parliament adopted the Divorce and Matrimonial Causes Act in 1857. That statute protected all of the property and earnings acquired by a wife from the moment her husband deserted her, and because it had not since been altered or repealed by either the colony or the Province of British Columbia, it was still the law on the BC mainland.

The British act did have one major drawback—a married woman had to wait two years before she could apply for a protection order. But that wasn't a problem in this case, because Mr. Cheffrey had deserted his wife six years earlier. Therefore, Begbie granted Maria a protection order under the Divorce and Matrimonial Causes Act, and all of her property was protected from her no-good husband and his creditors.

Consent Still Required

Until the adoption of the Married Women's Property Act in 1887, a married woman did not have the right to sell or otherwise dispose of her real property without her husband's consent. She couldn't even give it away in her will! And even after the law was enacted, a married woman still could not sell any real estate that was held in her name in trust for her husband. Thus, her spouse could continue to avoid his creditors by placing his real property in her name and be confident that she couldn't get rid of it.

But He's a Drunk

The Habitual Drunkards Act of 1887 allowed a wife to go to a jury to declare her spouse to be a "habitual drunkard" without any confirming medical opinion. The sale of alcohol to anyone who had been declared a habitual drunk was punishable by a $50 fine at that time. However, there is no recorded case of any woman taking advantage of this legislation. The reasons are rather simple. First, it involved hiring an attorney, which cost money. Second, if a husband was determined to be a habitual drunk, then he was not only prohibited from managing his estate, but also all of his financial affairs were placed in the hands of a trustee appointed by the provincial government (and there was no guarantee that the wife would get the job). Hubby would legally be considered a minor, which meant he couldn't sign contracts, among other things. Therefore, his spouse had to go to the trustee to get to his money or find a way to support herself, the couple's children and the drunkard husband!

Tough to Get Support

It wasn't until 1903 that a law in British Columbia made putative fathers financially responsible for their children. The Support of Illegitimate Children Act allowed anyone who furnished provisions and necessaries to an illegitimate child to go to court for a support order. However, before that could happen, the mother must have sworn an affidavit of paternity within six months of the child's birth or the possibility of getting support was forever lost. In addition, the law did not provide for the future support of a child; it only allowed for the reimbursement of monies already spent. As a result, the mother or whoever was taking care of the child (illegitimate children were frequently placed with private maternity boarding homes, charities and public facilities back then) would have had to return to court again and again at their own expense (lawyers, even in 1903, were not cheap) to seek compensation. The statute was thus rarely used. There were only three cases under the act in Vancouver between 1903 and 1914 and none at all in Victoria and New Westminster.

THE BOND BETWEEN FATHER AND CHILD

Who Gets to Raise the Kids?

Under a 1660 law, children of a married couple essentially belonged to the father. He alone had the power to determine the kids' education, religion and upbringing, and that power began from the moment of their conception. Dad also had the sole right to transfer the custody of his children (those who were under 21 years of age) to another person of his choosing through a deed or a will without the consent or prior knowledge of his wife. This even included any kids who were not yet born at the time of dad's death!

The Rights of Mothers

Did a mother have any rights as far as her children where concerned? Well, according to an 1839 statute, mom could seek custody of a child who was under seven years old, but even if she got it, the law required her to relinquish custody and hand the kid back to her husband or the child's guardian as soon as the youngster reached his or her seventh birthday! The law was changed in 1913 to allow a mother to keep the child after his or her seventh birthday (assuming mom was granted custody to begin with; mothers were rarely that lucky), but her husband still controlled the kid's property.

＊

Children

Kids, because of their youth and immaturity, have often been deemed to need extra legal protection that adults do not have. Some of the laws that were enacted in the past still make good sense today; others, because of what they did or did not regulate, might raise an eyebrow.

BANS ON DAYCARE AND HOUSING

How Long Am I Staying at the Babysitter's?

A 1901 provincial statute made it illegal for anyone to "retain or receive for hire or reward more than one infant, and, in the case of twins, more than two infants, under the age of one year, for the purpose of nursing or maintaining such infants apart from their parents for a longer period than twenty-four hours." The sole exception was when the nursing or care of the child occurred at a maternity boarding house that was registered with the local municipality.

No Room at the Inn

The same 1901 law also prohibited everyone except registered maternity boarding houses from providing room and board for a fee to unmarried mothers and their infants. So much for apartments and hotel rooms.

BAD HABITS
Don't Sell that Kid a Drink!

British Columbia's first Youths Protection Act, adopted in 1877, made it illegal for anyone with a retail or wholesale liquor licence to sell or give any alcohol to someone whom they had a "reasonable cause to believe…to be under the age of sixteen years." (Yes, 16!)

The law said nothing about other people (e.g., family, friends, a stranger leaving a bar) giving booze to minors. The statute also did not make it unlawful for a minor to possess or drink alcohol. It was believed that those matters were better left to parental authority rather than to government control.

The penalty for violating the law was a fine of up to $50 (almost $1000 in today's money) or up to one month in jail.

Can't Play Games Either
The 1877 statute also made it illegal for any saloon or barroom keeper or any vendor who sold alcohol to knowingly permit someone under 16, "other than his own child, ward or employé [sic]," to remain in a place where liquor was sold, or to allow the youngster to stay there and play "any game of cards, billiards, bagatelle or any other game."

Not in Vancouver

The 1877 provincial statute against selling booze to minors apparently wasn't good enough for Vancouver's city fathers. One of the city's first bylaws, adopted in 1886, made it illegal for any person to "sell or give any intoxicating drink to any child." The prohibition did not specify, however, at what age one was still considered to be a "child."

CASE FILE
Not Too Young to Be Spanked

Minors found in beer parlours in the 1920s initially faced no punishment—they were merely kicked out of the establishment and told never to return. But the law was changed in 1927 so that anyone under the drinking age who was discovered in a parlour was subject to a $300 fine or, if they couldn't pay, three months in jail.

During the height of the Great Depression in 1932, two underage lads from Kamloops were caught taking two young women to a beer parlour in Chase. Neither the boys nor their parents had the money to pay the fine and one lad supported his widowed mom. The provincial government got involved and reduced the fine to $50, but even that was too high. It was eventually decided that the sentence would be remitted if the boys agreed to be spanked "in the place provided by nature" by their parents while under the watchful eyes of the police. History does not record what happened to the young women, and it is not known if they were also underage or if they actually entered the beer parlour themselves.

No Selling Smokes to Minors

BC's first law regarding the use and sale of tobacco products was the Minor's Protection Act of 1891.

The statute made it a crime for anyone, including parents, to give or sell "any cigars, cigarettes, smoking or chewing tobacco, snuff or any other form or preparation of tobacco" to anyone under the age of 15. (The age was increased to 16 in 1902. It wasn't raised to 19 until 1994.)

The penalty for giving or selling tobacco to a minor was a $20 fine.

The law also made it illegal to give or sell opium to anyone under 15. (Opium was then a legal commodity.)

And, of course, it was against the law to buy or otherwise obtain tobacco products for someone who was under 15 in exchange for money "or any other valuable consideration."

Don't Smoke on the Street

The 1891 act also prohibited anyone under 15 from using tobacco on any public street, road, highway or building. If caught, the kid faced a $5 fine. Smoking at home or some-where else away from the public eye was okay. As with the 1877 statute dealing with youthful drinking, it was believed that those matters were better left to the parents.

Native Kids Can Smoke

The 1891 statute expressly did not apply to members of the First Nations. Apparently no one was very concerned about the lungs and health of Native children.

YOUNGSTERS' WORKING CONDITIONS

No Sweatshops for Children!

The first law in British Columbia regulating the working hours and conditions of minors was the Shops Regulation Act of 1900. The statute made it illegal for anybody under the age of 16 to work at "any retail or wholesale shop, store, booth, stall or warehouse" for more than 66½ hours per week. They were also not allowed to work for more than 13 hours on any Saturday or more than 11 hours on any other day (meal times included). Makes you wonder how long children had to work before the statute was enacted.

The statute further required that every employee under 16 be given not less than one hour for lunch and, if they worked beyond 7:00 PM, not less than 45 minutes for dinner.

The law did not apply, however, to kids working at a family-owned business run by their parents if the business was in or attached to their home.

What Is It About Bakeries?

There must have been something particularly dangerous about working in bakeries in the early 20th century. A 1901 amendment to the Shops Regulation Act not only prohibited anyone under 18 from working at a bakery between 9:00 PM and 5:00 AM, but it also banned everyone under 14 from being employed there.

Working in Industry

BC's Employment of Children Act of 1921 prohibited boys under the age of 14, and girls under 15, from working in any "public or private industrial undertaking" other than one in which only members of their family were employed.

Furthermore, while the statute specifically included mining and construction as industrial undertakings, it omitted from its provisions any work in the agricultural, horticultural and dairy industries.

The Apprentice

British Columbia's Apprentices and Minors Act, adopted in the late 1880s, allowed a dad to bind, with the consent of his boys, any of his sons who were 14 years of age or older as an apprentice to "any respectable and trustworthy master-mechanic, farmer or other person carrying on a trade or calling" for a term not to exceed the boy's 21st birthday.

A father could also, with the girl's permission, similarly bind any of his daughters, provided they were at least 12 years old, to "any respectable and trustworthy person carrying on any trade or calling, or to domestic service with any respectable and trustworthy person" until she turned 21.

A mother had the same power, but only after the father of her children had abandoned the kids and left them with her. Even then, mom (unlike dad) had to get the okay from two justices of the peace before she could act.

PROTECTING THE YOUNG'UNS

No Children Allowed!

Both the 1913 and 1914 versions of the Moving Pictures Act made it illegal for a theatre manager to permit anyone under the age of 14 to watch a film after 6:00 PM unless the child was accompanied by an adult. However, children were allowed in the theatre between 3:30 and 6:00 PM on school days and anytime before 6:00 PM on any other day.

Separate Cells

In the old days in British Columbia, if a child was arrested for a crime, he or she was thrown in jail with the adult prisoners. That changed with the Children's Protection Act of 1901, which stipulated that no one under the age of 15 could be "placed in the company of adult persons in any police lock-up or common gaol [i.e., jail], but shall be kept in a separate room or building."

You were still thrown in with the adults if you were 15 or older.

Curfew

A 1919 Vancouver bylaw made it illegal for any minor under the age of 16 "to be abroad upon any public place...unless accompanied by some adult person...or unless upon some errand upon the permission or direction of his parents, guardian or employer" between 9:00 PM and 6:00 AM.

The bylaw was changed in 1920 so minors could be "abroad" until 9:30 PM from April to October, but apparently having kids out so late during summer wasn't a good idea because the city went back to an all-year 9:00 PM to 6:00 AM curfew three years later. The Vancouver council also added a provision in 1923 making it illegal "for any parent or guardian to allow, suffer or permit any child under his care or control to be abroad or loiter upon any street within the City" between those hours. The penalty for letting your kid out late at night was a fine of up to $100 (almost $1250 in today's money) and up to two months in jail.

Education

A mind is a terrible thing to waste. But a glance into how much (or how little) schooling was required in the past as well as what was put into a student's noggin in the classroom might surprise you.

ATTENDANCE

You've Got to Go to School!

British Columbia was the second province in Canada to require children to go to school. (Ontario was the first.)

It began in 1873, one year after free education was brought to BC. Only kids between the ages of 7 and 14 had to attend class and, even then, it was for periods of time determined by the local school trustees, so there wasn't much uniformity across the province. Many trustees were reluctant to set specific requirements for when children had to be in school, and they often did not enforce their own decisions.

The Legislative Assembly tried to improve attendance in 1874 by making a teacher's pay dependent upon how many of his or her students actually showed up. As you can imagine, this did little to help enrolment and much to anger instructors.

The law was changed again in 1876. This time, all students between 7 and 12 (yes, 12!) were required to attend school for at least six months a year. The maximum age went back to 14 for students living in the cities in 1901 and for everyone else in 1912. The age was raised again, to 15, in 1921. It wasn't until 1990 that the maximum age was raised to 16.

But Only If You're Close to One

Under the Public School Act of 1905, children were required to attend classes only if there was a public school within 3 miles (5 kilometres) of their place of residence.

No Classroom Overcrowding

Under an 1885 statute, all high schools in BC had to have at least 20 students. Likewise, all elementary schools required at least 10, and all "assisted" schools (i.e., rural schools with less than 20 students that received financial aid from the province) needed only eight.

Not at Our School

One of the first things the Richmond School Board did after it was created in 1906 was to decide that only children whose parents owned real property could attend the district's public schools. This barred from the classroom the kids of Japanese immigrants whose families lived in houses owned by the canneries in Steveston.

RELIGION IN THE CLASSROOM

Prayer in School

The provincial Public School Act of 1872 stated:

> *All Public Schools established under the provisions of this Act, shall be conducted upon strictly non-sectarian principles. The highest morality shall be inculcated, but no religious dogmas or creed shall be taught.*

To strengthen the separation of church and state, another provision in the law prohibited the clergy from serving as teachers, school trustees or as the province's Superintendent of Education.

In 1891, the following sentence was added to the paragraph: "The Lord's Prayer may be used in opening or closing the School."

Still, British Columbia was the only province in Canada where Bible reading was not required at the beginning of the school day. That changed in 1944 when the law was amended:

> *All public schools shall be opened by the reading, without explanation or comment, of a passage of Scripture to be selected from readings prescribed or approved by the Council of Public Instruction. The reading of the passage of Scripture shall be followed by the recitation of the Lord's Prayer, but otherwise the schools shall be conducted on strictly secular and non-sectarian principles.*

Bible Readings No Longer Okay

In 1989, the BC Supreme Court held that the Bible readings and the recitation of the Lord's Prayer violated the students' constitutional right to freedom of conscience and religion under the Charter of Rights and Freedoms. Today, the School Act merely states that all schools:

> *...must be conducted on strictly secular and non-sectarian principles. The highest morality must be inculcated, but no religious dogma or creed is to be taught in a school or Provincial school.*

Sounds an awful lot like the 1872 statute, doesn't it?

TEST TIME!

Who Was that King Again?

Until 1938, all students wishing to attend high school in British Columbia were required to pass an entrance examination. The first exams, in 1876, covered arithmetic, geography, grammar and spelling, but it didn't take long before they included much more. And the questions weren't easy either!

The following were some of the questions on the 1898 exam regarding English grammar:

- Write a trisyllable, stating which are the stopped letters in it.

- Write the possessive plural feminine of "husband," "earl," "he," "sir" and "hart."

- Give the imperative mood, passive voice, of the verbs "do" and "be," and the infinitives of the passive voice of the verb "go."

- Define "ellipsis."

- How do you ascertain the antecedent of an interrogative pronoun?

And if you think that was a snap, try the following questions about British history:

☛ When and by whom was the conquest of Britain completed by the Romans?

☛ For what is each of the following kings noted: Egbert, Alfred, Edward the Confessor?

☛ When and through whom was the House of Commons founded?

☛ Give an account of the battles of Bannockburn and Agincourt.

☛ Name the sovereigns of the Stuart line with dates.

☛ Describe the Habeas Corpus Act.

☛ Name the five greatest warriors of Britain, stating at least one victory achieved by each.

How would you have done on this test?

That's One Long Exam!

The exam to get into high school wasn't something that you could take in just one hour. Check out the subjects covered in 1920 and the allotted test time for each:

☛ Dictation and Spelling: 1¼ hours

☛ Drawing: 2¼ hours

☛ English Literature: 2 hours

☛ Grammar and Composition: 2 hours

☛ Math: 2¼ hours

☛ Nature Lessons: 1½ hours

It's All Greek to Me

BC's high schools were originally intended to be the training grounds for the province's elementary school teachers. The following is an excerpt from a 19th-century high school curriculum in the province:

- ☛ English: ancient and modern geography, grammar, rhetoric and composition, mythology

- ☛ Scientific: botany, physiology, natural philosophy, astronomy, chemistry

- ☛ Mathematical: arithmetic, algebra, mensuration, Euclid [a type of geometry] and bookkeeping

- ☛ Classical: Latin and Greek

- ☛ Modern Languages: French

There were also mandatory courses in map making and vocal music. Commercial classes, besides bookkeeping, were added later (1901) as were manual training (i.e., practical arts and crafts, such as woodworking; 1908), domestic science (1909) and home economics (1917).

Business

Businesses have never been totally unregulated, but once things like minimum wages, working conditions and licence fees came into the picture, all sorts of peculiar statutes and bylaws were written.

MINIMUM WAGE
For Her, Not Him

British Columbia was the first province in Canada to enact a minimum wage law. The Minimum Wage Act of 1918, however, did not set a single wage that applied to everyone. In fact, it applied only to women. A minimum wage law for men was not adopted for another seven years, and there were two different minimum wage statutes for the sexes until BC's first unisex minimum wage law was enacted in 1972.

Only $12.75 per Week!

The Minimum Wage Act of 1918 also did not establish a uniform wage for all women in the province. Instead, the statute established a three-member Minimum Wage Board that divided workers into nine categories (mercantile, manufacturing, office occupations and so forth). The board then sent questionnaires to the employees inquiring about their yearly expenses (food, clothing, etc.) and to employers about the number of workers they hired and the wages paid. With this information, the board was to determine a minimum wage, as well as the maximum hours and working conditions, for each category.

However, before reaching its final decision, the Minimum Wage Board was required to hold "conferences" at which representatives of the employers, employees and the "disinterested public" would consider the evidence and recommend a minimum wage "adequate to supply the necessary cost of living." In reality, these conferences were bargaining negotiations, and the compromises that were reached often fell short of a subsistence wage. The board did not have to accept the recommendations, but it usually did.

For example, the questionnaires submitted by employees in the mercantile industry indicated that their average cost of living was $16.81 a week. The employers at the conference did not dispute that figure; they simply refused to pay it. Some even thought that $5 a week was more than fair! In the end, the conference recommended $12.75 a week for a 48-hour workweek, which the Minimum Wage Board approved.

Butlers and Maids

The Minimum Wage Act of 1918 and the Male Minimum Wage Act of 1925 did not apply to domestic servants. (The province's minimum wage laws did not apply to them until 1981!)

For that matter, the statutes also did not apply to farm labourers or fruit pickers. And while the 1918 law covered female cannery workers, their male counterparts were left out of the 1925 statute.

Too Young to Earn a Decent Wage

Most of the provisions of the Minimum Wage Act of 1918 did not apply to women under the age of 18. Instead, a special section in the law allowed the Minimum Wage Board to investigate and "determine wages and conditions of labour suitable for such girls" without the need for a "conference" of employees and employers. For these women, the board typically established graduated wages scales that increased over a one or two year period, but even at the end of the period the top wage was usually less than the minimum wage set for older women. And there was originally no limit as to how many underage women one could hire.

Cheap Female Labour

According to BC law, an employer could pay less than the minimum wage to inexperienced female apprentices who were over 18 years of age as well as to women who were "physically defective." An employer had to get a special licence from the Minimum Wage Board to hire these women at the lower rate. The number of women who could be paid at this reduced wage could not exceed 10 percent of the total number of females working at the particular store, factory or other establishment.

The number of female employees who could be hired under the special licence was increased to one-seventh, or roughly 14 percent, in 1921. That same year, the total number of women working at a business who either had the special licence or were under 18 was set at 35 percent.

Cheap Male Labour

Unlike its female counterpart, the Male Minimum Wage Act of 1925 applied only to adults; there was nothing in it about a minimum wage for men under 21. There were no limits either as to how many underage men an employer could hire.

A Way Out of the Law

Despite their role in the conferences that set the minimum wage, employers still tried to find ways to pay their employees less. Take the manufacturing industry, for example. The minimum wage for women in that field was set at $14 a week for a 44-hour week—they only worked four hours instead of eight on Saturdays, according to the orders of the Minimum Wage Board. But then the employers realized that another law, the Factories Act, allowed them to deduct $1.25 for the four hours that their employees would have otherwise worked on Saturday if it wasn't for the Minimum Wage Board's order. So, the employees' salaries were cut from $14 to $12.75 a week.

Yankee Dollars

With the sudden influx of tens of thousands of Americans into Victoria on their way to the Fraser River Gold Rush, U.S. dollars were suddenly all over the place. So, on April 7, 1859, the Legislative Assembly of Vancouver Island passed a law making American currency legal tender in the colony.

How Much for a Pound?

BC had its own currency before it joined Confederation in 1871. The mainland Colony of British Columbia abandoned the British pound for the BC dollar in 1865; Vancouver Island had adopted a decimal system two years earlier. And though it had not yet officially abandoned the pound, the mainland colony issued a few $10 and $20 coins as well as some $5, $10 and $25 notes in 1862. In addition, it was common in the 1860s for banks on both Vancouver Island and the mainland to issue their own paper money.

BC never issued any small coins, but pennies and other pocket change from the British colonies in eastern Canada were also in circulation as well as those from Great Britain and the United States. There were so many coins in fact that, in 1867, the BC Legislative Council (the colonial legislature after the mainland and Vancouver Island were merged into one) passed a law making American and British coinage legal tender and set a rate of exchange.

American coins were worth their face value, but an entire schedule was laid out for the conversion of British coins:

Pound sterling, or sovereign	$4.85
Half-sovereign	$2.42½
Crown piece	$1.25
Shilling	$0.25
Sixpence	$0.12½
Threepenny	$0.06

WORKING CONDITIONS
Please Sit Down

British Columbia's Shops Regulation Act of 1900 contained a number of revolutionary ideas. For example, it required all employers to keep "a sufficient and suitable seat or chair" for the use of every one of their female employees (one employee to one chair) and "to permit her to use such seat or chair when not necessarily engaged in the work or duty for which she is employed." This law did not apply to a family-owned business that was in or attached to the family's home.

Workplace Sanitation

Under the same Shops Regulation Act of 1900, employees at retail or wholesale businesses were entitled under the law to "a sufficient number and description of privies, earth- or water-closets and urinals" that must "at all times be kept clean and well ventilated." Hate to think of what they had to do when nature called before the law was enacted.

Stay Home!

One of the first laws in British Columbia concerning parental leave was the Maternity Protection Act of 1921. Under that statute, it was illegal for any woman to work (even if she wanted to) at any "public or private industrial or commercial undertaking" during the six weeks following the birth of her child. Once she was back at work, she could nurse her baby for half an hour, twice a day, during her work hours.

The statute defined a woman as "any female person, irrespective of age or nationality, whether married or unmarried." It's interesting that BC's provincial legislators felt they had to mention age, nationality and marital status when explaining what a woman is.

What Was Going on Before 1901?

A provincial statute was adopted in 1901 containing regulations that dealt specifically with the working conditions in British Columbia's bakeries.

All bakeshops now had to have sufficient lighting, heating, ventilation and "draining" to not be "detrimental or injurious to the health of any person working therein." They also had to be kept in a "clean and sanitary condition, so as to secure the production and preservation of all the food products therein in a good and wholesome condition." There was even a clause in the statute that specifically required all bakeries to have a washroom and another that mandated every bakery to have "proper means and facilities of escape in case of fire." And it was no longer legal for bakeries to operate out of cellars or "underground."

No Sleeping on the Job

Beginning in 1901, no one was allowed to sleep in a BC bakery, and any place intended for employees to sleep had to be entirely separated from the bakeshop.

Furthermore, no employee was permitted to work in a bakeshop for more than 12 hours on any day or 60 hours in any week without the employer first getting special written permission from a government inspector.

YOU NEED A LICENCE FOR THAT!

Astrologers v. Lawyers

Like other municipalities, Nanaimo has, from time to time, set the fees to be charged whenever a business licence is issued. In 1897, every astrologer and fortune teller had to pay $25 (or about $640 in today's money) every six months, but lawyers and solicitors had to pay only $12.50.

It's Gonna Cost Ya!

The Delta City Council set out in 1884 the fees to be charged for various licences. Every licence was good for only six months and, of course, another fee had to be paid to get it renewed.

By far the most highly priced was the $250 (almost $5900 today) licence required to sell opium (which was then legal in Canada). Chemists and druggists who used the drug when preparing medical prescriptions didn't need one, but everyone else did. And you had to buy a $5 licence if you wanted to smoke opium.

The runner-up for most expensive licence was the $30 one required of retail liquor merchants. Auctioneers, except for the sheriff and other government employees, needed a $10 licence. And finally, while all retail merchants and "every commercial traveller following his calling" needed a $5 licence, peddlers and hawkers had to pay $10.

When Opium Was Legal

Under an 1886 Vancouver bylaw, anyone could manufacture, sell, barter, exchange or otherwise traffic in opium in any form so long as they paid $500 a year for a licence from the city. Again, duly qualified chemists or druggists who used the drug to prepare a doctor's prescription didn't need a licence.

It was cheaper for opium manufacturers and dealers to do business in Victoria (where 13 opium factories operated in 1888). An opium licence in Victoria cost only $100 a year until 1886, when the fee was increased to $250 per annum. Nanaimo also profited from the sale of opium licence fees. And the federal government took in over $1 million in custom duties charged on opium that was imported into British Columbia between 1872 and 1900.

It was not until 1908 that opium became illegal in Canada.

PoCo Shuts Down Lemonade Stand

Port Coquitlam, like most communities, has a bylaw requiring businesses to get a licence before they set up shop in a city park. Minors are not exempt from its provisions.

But two 12-year-olds did not know that when they opened up a stand in Shaughnessy Park's off-leash area in August 2010 to sell lemonade, popcorn and homemade puppy treats. Their intent was to raise money for new uniforms for their soccer team, but after a couple of weeks somebody complained, and the city's bylaw enforcement officers shut the stand down.

In a way, it was all for the best. The boys soon found themselves on national TV, and when they re-opened their lemonade stand (this time, on mom's front lawn), they had earned in one day over half of the $1000 they were trying to raise for their teammates.

ABOVE THE LAW
Must Write in English

The BC Legislative Assembly passed a statute in 1907 making it unlawful for any business to employ someone who could not write in a European language. However, the province's lieutenant-governor, James Dunsmuir, who himself employed a large number of Chinese Canadians who could not read or write in English, refused to give royal assent. His lack of action led directly to a race riot in Vancouver.

CASE FILE
Too Important to Retire!

Ernest Cleveland, the first chief commissioner of the Greater Vancouver Water Board, had been on the job since 1926 and nobody wanted to lose him after he turned 65 on May 12, 1939. But Cleveland had reached the mandatory retirement age set out in BC's Municipal Superannuation Act of 1938.

The solution? The Legislative Assembly passed a law in December 1940 that specifically exempted Cleveland and his fellow commissioners from the provisions of the 1938 act. It also allowed them to remain in office until the Water Board decided to fire them or until they retired.

Cleveland stayed on for another 12 years. The Cleveland Dam on Capilano River is named after him. And he's also probably the only man in BC history for whom an entire law was written.

Tax the Carriage Trade

There existed in downtown Victoria in the early 20th century a high-class "carriage trade" prostitution business that served the city's elite. Because prostitution was illegal, the city fathers couldn't tax the establishments or require the women to obtain a business licence, so these houses of prostitution were raided twice a year and fined $100. It was seen as part of the cost of doing business and gave the municipality a vested interest in the houses' success, which led City Hall and the police to ignore the occasional complaints that were made about them.

Sunday
Blue Laws

Sunday was once considered, and still is by many, to be a special day of rest. But the idea that everyone had to rest on Sunday was once part of the law. And only certain kinds of R&R were permitted. Many activities that people engage in today to relax and recuperate were actually banned on that "day of rest."

WHAT YOU CAN AND CAN'T DO ON SUNDAY

No Fun on the Lord's Day

The Lord's Day Act was adopted by Parliament in 1906. The statute prohibited across Canada the occurrence of most business transactions and recreational activities on Sunday. Based on various laws that had been in effect in England since the 15th century, the act was meant to turn back what many felt was the increasing secularization of the Sabbath and to compel Canadians to observe Sunday as a Christian holy day.

Almost everything that involved the exchange of money or other gain was banned; you couldn't even catch up on paperwork or restock your store's shelves! It was also illegal to attend or provide any entertainment (sports, movies, concerts, you name it) other than at a church, and it didn't matter if it was just you and your friends getting together to play some street hockey or an event you had to buy a ticket for.

There were, of course, a number of exceptions in the law for "works of necessity and mercy," such as providing and selling medicine and the delivery of milk, and for businesses in the tourism sector, like hotels and restaurants. And the statute contained "opt-out" provisions that allowed any province to list even more exemptions.

In addition to the federal Lord's Day Act, British Columbia had its own Sunday observance law. However, it applied only to the mainland and was never in effect on Vancouver Island.

No Bull-baiting, Picnics or Baseball on the Mainland!

When the Colony of British Columbia was established on November 19, 1858, all English laws that existed on that date were to apply to the new colony. Some doubts arose, however, as to whether this included England's Sunday observance statutes, so a proclamation was issued on May 18, 1863, making it clear that they were indeed part of BC's law.

The proclamation was turned into a statute when the colonies of British Columbia and Vancouver Island merged into one in 1866. However, a clause was added specifying that the law applied only to mainland BC, and it remained there for over three-quarters of a century after British Columbia joined Confederation. Furthermore, five old English statutes were incorporated into BC's Sunday observance law, including one that dated from 1625, which had the lengthy name of "An Act for punishing Divers Abuses committed on the Lord's Day, called Sunday." That statute said:

> …there shall be no meetings, assemblies, or concourse of people outside their parishes on the Lord's Day…for any sports and pastimes whatsoever; nor any bear-baiting, bull-baiting, interludes [or] common plays…by any person or persons within their own parishes.

Violators were fined a penalty of three shillings four pence (or about $470 in today's money), which was to be given to the poor. If the offender didn't have the cash, then his land and property were to be sold, and if that didn't satisfy the debt, then he was to be "set publicly in the stocks by the space of three hours."

There's no record of anyone in British Columbia being set out in the stocks for bull-baiting, having a picnic, playing baseball or doing any other activity on a Sunday.

The Supreme Court of Canada held in 1959 that BC's Sunday Observance Act became ineffective upon the adoption of the new federal Criminal Code in 1953.

No Haircuts
Nanaimo adopted a bylaw in 1899 closing all local barbershops on Sunday. You had to wait and let your hair grow a little longer if you forgot to get it chopped off on Saturday.

No Concerts or Movies!
As time passed, British Columbians wanted to do more on Sunday than just stay at home or go to church.

A delegation of women from the British Progressive League even complained to the Vancouver City Council in 1924. They argued that if one alderman was allowed to sell ice cream and another to fill prescriptions on Sunday, then their members should be able to attend concerts on that day as well. But the council gave them the cold shoulder. After all, as the women were told, if theatres were permitted to hold concerts on Sunday, then that "would be the thin edge of the wedge" toward opening movie theatres on Sunday too!

You Want to Get Buried When?

A 1953 Vancouver bylaw banned all burials on Sundays and statutory holidays at the city-owned Mountain View Cemetery. Such burials were previously allowed only with the approval of the mayor, who granted permission to some religious groups but not to others.

Quiet Evenings

It is illegal to use a power saw in Oak Bay after 7:00 PM except for Sundays (when you're not allowed to use it at all).

So Much for Valuing Your Constituents' Wishes
A petition with 56,000 signatures asking for a city-wide referendum on whether or not to allow people to go to movies on Sunday was presented to the Vancouver City Council in 1961.

Alderwoman Marianne Linnell, however, just fluffed it off. "It's a lot of eyewash," she said. "We have to take them [i.e., the signatures] with a grain of salt because people signed it [the petition] without really thinking about it." Religious leaders appearing before the council also opposed the idea. One United Church minister said that "matters of moral and spiritual principal can't be decided by voters" (as if paying to see a movie on Sunday, as opposed to seeing it for free on TV, might endanger one's soul), and a Baptist leader said that most films "are unfit for weekdays, let alone Sundays." In fact, the entire city council rejected the idea and unanimously voted to kill the proposal.

CASE FILE
Burnaby v. Vancouver

The Burnaby City Council was screaming mad in 1964. Its residents were not allowed to play sports or see a film on Sunday while those in Vancouver could. (Vancouver repealed its no Sunday movies bylaw in '63.) The Burnaby council asked the provincial government to at least amend the Municipal Act so local communities could decide for themselves whether to open up Sundays to fun. Other British Columbians agreed. The residents of Penticton voted in a referendum to allow bowling on Sunday, and Richmond's gave the thumbs-up to allowing athletic and cultural events and movies. There was also agitation for local plebiscites in New Westminster and West Vancouver. But everyone had to wait because Premier W.A.C. Bennett, Attorney General Robert Bonner and most of the Social Credit Party (Socred) caucus in the provincial legislature (the right-wing Social Credit Party then held a large majority in the Legislative Assembly) opposed opening Sunday to sports and other entertainment.

One Step Backward

BC Municipal Affairs Minister Dan Campbell wanted in 1964 to re-impose on Vancouver the ban on Sunday entertainment. Fortunately, the city bylaw that was adopted in 1958 to allow Sunday sports said that the bylaw could not be rescinded without there first being a majority vote in favour of repeal in a city-wide plebiscite.

No Sunday Shopping Until 1980

Although Sunday entertainment became legal throughout British Columbia in 1969, Sunday shopping still was not.

The BC Legislative Assembly adopted the Holiday Shopping Regulation Act in 1980 to opt out of the Lord's Day Act and to leave the legality of Sunday shopping to the municipalities. This included not only individual stores and shopping malls, but also entertainment businesses that charged for admission, such as movie theatres, museums and concerts.

Coquitlam, Richmond, Vancouver and Victoria quickly deregulated Sunday retail hours in 1981. Maple Ridge followed suit in 1985 and Chilliwack in 1990. Abbotsford and Langley simply no longer bothered to enforce the Lord's Day Act despite the lack of any formal bylaw deregulating Sunday shopping.

Can't Sell Booze

The first ban in BC against selling alcohol at a specific time or on a particular day was enacted in 1891.

The Liquor License Regulation Act prohibited the sale of alcoholic beverages on Sundays or, to be more exact, from 11:00 PM Saturday until 1:00 AM Monday. The statute also permitted local municipal councils to ban liquor sales at other hours during the week, but otherwise booze could still be sold 24/7.

However, the Sunday ban did not apply to the "furnishing of liquor to bonâ fide travelers [sic]," so anyone who was willing to travel at least 3 miles (5 kilometres) could still get a drink. The law proved rather ineffective since it did not require bars to be locked or have their lights out on Sundays.

Shopping

Many people like to shop. But when? How about Wednesday? Nope, can't do it. It's against the law. Saturday night? Uh-uh. That's illegal too. How about the day after Boxing Day? Forget it.

The fact is, now that many stores are open seven days a week and often late into the night (with a few open 24/7), it might seem odd that there were once very strict laws requiring businesses to close at absurdly early hours—and sometimes for entire days.

BUSINESS HOURS

Closed for Christmas

The Shops Regulation Act of 1900 gave municipal councils the power to require all local businesses, or any particular type of business, to close at an hour set by the council provided that the appointed time was not before 6:00 PM.

The law was amended two years later so that municipal councils could require businesses to be closed all day on statutory holidays. (Before this, any Scrooge in British Columbia could make Bob Cratchit work on Christmas Day.)

Not Too Late to Get Flowers for Mom!

Vancouver's 1930 closing bylaw allowed most retail businesses to be open only from 6:00 AM to 6:00 PM. However, there were a number of exceptions.

For example, vegetable dealers and retail grocers could remain open until 9:00 PM. Flower shops could also stay open until that time and could even keep their doors open until 10:00 PM the days immediately before Good Friday, Easter Sunday and Mother's Day.

Stores could be open until midnight so long as they sold only fresh fruit and confectionary (which was defined in the bylaw to include biscuits, cakes, breads, candy and sweetmeats, gum, soft drinks and dairy products). They could also stay open 24 hours to sell medicines, drugs, medical appliances, toilet requirements, photographic supplies and "pharmaceutical rubber goods." Exceptions were also made for service stations and auto repair shops.

All other stores had to obtain a special licence if they wanted to remain open all day and night. Every store could stay open until 10:00 PM on Christmas Eve but had to be closed on statutory holidays. Finally, the bylaw did not apply to taverns, hotels, restaurants, pawnbrokers or tobacconists.

How Late Can I Shop?

The BC Legislative Assembly decided in 1957 that all "shops" across the province had to close no later than 6:00 PM at least four nights a week. Furthermore, unless a local municipal council specified otherwise, the 6:00 PM witching hour applied to Monday, Tuesday, Thursday and Saturday.

Likewise, unless a municipal council picked another day, all stores had to close every Wednesday no later than noon. Whether it was Wednesday or another day they picked for the weekly half-holiday, municipal councils were allowed to let the shops stay open on that day until 6:00 PM in July and August.

Finally, again unless a local municipal council picked another day, all stores could remain open until 9:00 PM on Fridays.

Of course, "shops" were defined only as those places where a retail trade or business was carried on and did not include establishments such as hotels and restaurants.

UNIQUE AND FORGOTTEN HOLIDAYS

Wrestling Day

Williams Lake is probably the only place in the world that celebrates Wrestling Day every January 2.

Two local merchants on January 2, 1938, discovered that neither of them had any customers all morning long. The pair got on the phone, called the other businesses in town and learned that they too had no patrons during the day. Everyone promptly agreed that it was a good time to declare a holiday, close their doors and go home.

The informal holiday became a city tradition and, on December 23, 1942, Williams Lake's Village Commission declared January 2 as a civic holiday. A city bylaw was adopted in 1959 to make it a legal statutory holiday so the local banks would have to close.

Wrestling Day was briefly abolished in 1977. Mayor Tom Manson said that Williams Lake had outgrown such nonsense. It's just as likely that the action was taken because the big chain stores that had recently come to Williams Lake, as well as some of the local unionized lumber mills, neither appreciated nor recognized the holiday. Cancelling Wrestling Day, however, caused such a public fury that the city council reversed its decision the following year.

And the origin of the name? Some say one of those merchants back in 1938 figured that if the day after Christmas was Boxing Day, then the day after New Year's should be called Wrestling Day. Others say that the moniker was picked because half the town was still wrestling every January 2 with a hangover from all the drinking they did on New Year's Eve.

In the Beginning...

A peculiar retail tradition that existed in British Columbia for over a half century was the half-holiday.

The Shops Regulation Act of 1900 gave municipal councils the power to establish a "half-holiday" on any day of the week. Specifically, each municipal council could require all businesses, or all shops within a particular type of business (e.g., barbershops or watchmakers) to close for half a day on a particular day of the week at a time not earlier than noon. Of course, there were a number of exceptions to the statute where such a holiday would make no sense, including hotels and restaurants. Also excluded were bars, tobacconist shops, auction rooms, pawnbrokers and stores where second-hand goods and wares were bought and sold.

The half-holiday must have been popular because in 1916 the provincial legislature made it mandatory. Now every incorporated city, town, township and district municipality had to adopt bylaws requiring all local businesses to close every Wednesday or Saturday afternoon (which day was the municipality's choice) at a time no later than 1:00 PM. Furthermore, no employer could require or permit any of his employees to remain at the store for more than 30 minutes after closing. The penalty for staying open or having your employees stick around after hours was $10 for the first offence, $50 for the second and $100 for the third and all subsequent violations. (That's nearly $200, $1000 and $2000 in today's money.)

Wednesday or Saturday?

The Weekly Half-Holiday Act of 1916 mandated city-wide elections in New Westminster, Vancouver and Victoria so the voters could decide for themselves whether the half-holiday would occur on Wednesday or Saturday. In all other communities, the local municipal councils made the decision or, if they failed to do so, the individual employers and their employees had to decide on the day for themselves (and so one store might be closed on Wednesday while their neighbours were closed on Saturday).

The statute did not apply to the unincorporated areas within the province.

The electorate in Vancouver originally voted in 1916 to have their half-holiday on Saturdays but changed their mind and went for Wednesdays a year later. Voters in New Westminster and Victoria also picked Wednesday.

CASE FILE
Outlaws

New Year's Day was one of those legal holidays when all businesses in Vancouver had to be closed. New Year's Eve in 1941 fell on a Wednesday, and some local retailers defied the half-holiday law by staying open beyond 1:00 PM. As said by George Matthews, the Secretary-Treasurer of the Retail Merchants Association, the decision was not "based on making extra money but rather on furnishing an absolutely necessary service." Yeah, right.

Half-holidays Turn into Full Holidays

The BC legislature amended the half-holiday law in 1946 and 1947 so that municipal councils could turn half-holidays into full-day holidays.

There were two ways to do this. First, under the '46 statute, a local council could adopt a full-day holiday for a particular type of business if three-quarters of the owners of those businesses petitioned for one. Second, under the '47 act, each council could, on its own discretion, require all local businesses, or all shops within a particular type of business, to be closed one whole day during the week.

All-day closing was rejected in 1947 by the Victoria city council by a vote of seven to four. (The city's electors defeated an all-day closing proposal in a plebiscite the previous December by two to one.) The Kamloops city council approved a bylaw for an all-day holiday every Wednesday, but it was stricken down by the court because the council didn't properly follow the procedure laid out in the provincial statute.

But in Vancouver—WOW! Over 100,000 people signed a petition that was sent to Vancouver City Hall in favour of closing all of the city's stores for an entire day on Wednesday. The city council, however, refused to make a decision and went instead for a city-wide election on the subject.

Vancouverites approved in a 1947 plebiscite the full-day closing of stores by 20,317 to 12,051, but only one in four qualified voters bothered to cast a ballot.

After the vote, the Vancouver City Council promptly divided all of the city's retail establishments into 37 categories (everything from boot and shoe dealers to hobby supply stores) and issued a series of bylaws making it illegal for any of them to be open on Wednesdays.

Kill the Full-day Holiday

Until 1986, it was illegal in Vancouver for a stove dealer to do business on a Wednesday.

Why, you ask. Well, it goes back to the old full-day holiday law.

The BC Legislative Assembly passed a statute in 1954 allowing Vancouver to adopt a bylaw to permit six full days of shopping. (The federal Lord's Day Act prohibited retail stores from being open on Sunday.) The law applied only to Vancouver; all other communities in the province were still required to have a half-day holiday every week.

The statute required Vancouver to first have a plebiscite on the matter. No problem. On June 23, 1954, Vancouverites voted 36,363 to 31,149 (but with only 39.7 percent of the eligible voters going to the polls) to abolish the full-day Wednesday closing and have six full days to shop.

The second requirement was that more than half of the owners of a particular type of business had to petition the Vancouver City Council for a six-day week before the council could give them one.

Almost immediately, merchants from 30 of the 37 categories set out by the Vancouver City Council in 1947 petitioned the city council to have the Wednesday shopping ban thrown out. However, whether because of laziness or lack of support, no petitions were ever presented on behalf of the following businesses:

☛ Retail art dealers

☛ Retail electrical appliance dealers

☛ Retail paints and wallpaper dealers

☛ Retail stove dealers

☛ Retail tent and awning dealers

☛ Retail window blind dealers

☛ Watch repair shops

It wasn't until 1986 that the Vancouver City Council finally got around to repealing the all-day Wednesday closing bylaw. The regulation had long since been forgotten, but it was still technically in place. So, it was technically still illegal for a stove dealer to do business on a Wednesday.

ACROSS THE BORDER
Shop Duty-free in the USA

To encourage settlement, the federal government allowed Surrey residents in the late 19th century to buy their supplies duty-free at stores on the American side of the international border provided that they informed Customs twice a year about their purchases.

At the time, the only Canadian stores with a supply of goods large enough to meet Surrey's needs were in New Westminster and Victoria, but it was much more difficult for a Surreyite to reach either of those cities than it was to get to Bellingham or Blaine in Washington. For example, the distance from Halls Prairie (a neighbourhood of Surrey near present-day White Rock) to New West was 16 kilometres while Blaine was just a stone's throw away.

In addition, until 1904 there were no bridges across the Fraser River that connected Surrey with New Westminster; in fact, there wasn't even a ferry service until 1883. And once the ferry was established, the price of passage could quickly empty any poor Surrey farmer's pocket. (The charges ranged from 10 cents—about $2.25 today—for every calf, sheep, pig and child to $1 for an ox-team and $2.50 for a threshing machine with attachments and accompanying horses.)

Entertainment

Who says that British Columbia is no fun? Any place that once prohibited boisterous dancing, jiu jitsu and walkathons can't be all bad!

MUST-SEE MOVIES AND BANNED CONCERTS

You've Got to See this Picture!

The provincial government established the British Columbia Patriotic and Educational Picture Service (PEPS) in 1919 to increase local film production. And to ensure a market for the organization's theatrical shorts, the BC legislature passed a law the following year requiring all movie theatres in the province to show at least one of the PEPS' 10-minute educational films and travelogues every day. Talk about a captive audience!

Only Shakespeare Allowed

One of the first bylaws regulating theatres and theatrical
productions in Vancouver was adopted in 1907. It contained
a provision that banned the presentation of "any amusement,
concert or entertainment other than theatrical and dramatic
exhibitions" at any theatre unless permission was first
obtained from the city council. The mayor's okay alone,
however, was sufficient if you wanted to use the stage "for
public meetings for propaganda or political purposes."

CAN'T HAVE TOO MUCH FUN

No Sparklers

White Rock prohibits the sale and discharge of fireworks. Port Moody isn't quite as strict; you are allowed to shoot off fireworks on Halloween night but only if you're at least 18 years of age, and only from your yard. Setting them off in a street or in a park is a no-no.

No Loud Celebrations

An 1887 Vancouver bylaw prohibited the firing of any guns "or other firearms" within the city.

You also could not shoot off any fireworks, fireballs, crackers, squibs, serpents or "any other noisy, offensive or dangerous substantives" or "make or light any fire in any of the streets, squares, parks or public places" in Vancouver without first getting the okay from the mayor or city council.

Finally, whether you had permission or not, no fireworks or bonfires were allowed "in any place where or near which there is any crowd or assemblage of people or where there are any animals liable to be frightened nearby."

So much for Canada Day, Halloween and New Year's Day!

No Fun in Langley!

The Township of Langley must have been full of fuddy-duddies in 1911. The town council that year made it illegal on Sunday, and on any "public highway or lanes" within the municipality during the entire week, to "discharge any gun or firearm of any description or to fire or set off fireballs, squibs, crackers or fireworks of any kind or description." Violating the bylaw would cost you $25 (or over $560 today).

CASE FILE
No Boisterous Dancing?

Vancouver Licence Inspector H.A. Urquhart bragged in November 1943 that he, during the previous few months, used the city's licence bylaw (which gave him the unilateral power to grant, deny and revoke business licences) to eliminate "boisterous dancing to juke box music" in more than a dozen hamburger and soft drink establishments.

SPORTS

Jiu-jitsu

Vancouver passed a bylaw in 1907 making it illegal for anyone to engage in jiu-jitsu or for anyone to encourage or promote any jiu-jitsu contest. The penalty was a fine of up to $100 or up to two months in jail.

Can't Walk Here

In the 1930s, walkathons were the latest craze and were often held at Vancouver's many theatres, but the provincial Attorney General called them "outrageous" and the most "nonsensical thing I've ever heard of." The provincial health officer thought they were a danger to the participants' health and sanity, and local church groups said they were immoral and indecent. So the Vancouver City Council voted in a special session on July 3, 1931, to ban all walkathons after July 23. The three-week delay was allowed so that two previously scheduled walkathons could go on; otherwise, the theatres that had already obtained the necessary licences might sue. Still, there were city councillors who preferred to go to trial and pay whatever penalties would be imposed if the city lost in court rather than allow the walkathons to go on.

Censorship

Censorship has often been used under the guise of protecting public morality. But as the saying goes, "one man's trash is another man's treasure." Let's see just how far the law went to keep the "garbage" out of the province.

AT THE CINEMA

Forget Abbott and Costello!

Imagine that you're back in 1948 and want to catch the movie *Abbott and Costello Meet Frankenstein*. Or it's 1915 and you plan to see Charlie Chaplin's *His Night Out*. You'd be out of luck because both movies were banned in British Columbia.

The provincial legislature adopted the Moving Pictures Act in 1913. That statute created the office of the "Censor" and gave the person holding that position and his assistants the duty to examine all films proposed to be shown in British Columbia and the power to prohibit their exhibition in order to prevent:

> the depiction of scenes of an immoral or obscene nature, the representation of crime or pictures reproducing any brutalizing spectacle, or which indicate or

*suggest lewdness or indecency, or the infidelity or
unfaithfulness of husband or wife, or any other such
pictures which he may consider injurious to morals
or against the public welfare or which may offer evil
suggestions to the minds of children, or which may be
likely to offend the public.*

The Legislative Assembly replaced the 1913 law with another
Moving Pictures Act in 1914, but the above wording was
retained and it remained unchanged until 1970, when the
modern film classification and rating system was put into place.

Censor's Word Was Law

Beginning in 1914, the censor also had the power to deny
a business licence to, or revoke the licence of, any movie theatre in the province at "his discretion." Furthermore, the law
had no procedures by which to "un-ban" a film and, until
1929, there was no way to appeal the censor's decision, so for
a while, whether a movie could be seen by the public was subject to the censor's whim and his word was law.

Going a Little Overboard

NO US FLAGS OR WOMEN SMOKING CIGARETTES
One of the first movies to fall victim was 1914's *In the
Clutches of Gangsters.* It was rejected because of its "unneces-
sary display of US flags and excessive depiction of crime."
Another movie from that period, *The Baby* was kept out of
BC theatres because it contained "nine scenes of wanton
women smoking cigarettes." In 1920, *River's End* was prohib-
ited because it was deemed an "unpleasant reflection on [the]
Royal Canadian Mounted Police." The 1925 Russian film
Battleship Potemkin, artistically one of the most important
films of all time, was banned as "communistic propaganda."

YOU CAN'T KISS HER!
Romances were targets if their characters did not conform to traditional values. For example, an early Humphrey Bogart–Myrna Loy film, *Body and Soul* (1931), was described by the censor as the "story of a decent cultured woman putting herself in [the] position of her late husband's mistress" and was prohibited because "her action of free love smacks too much of the doctrine of free love as practiced in Soviet Russia." The 1933 Spencer Tracy romantic tragedy, *Man's Castle*, was banned because of its detrimental effect upon "young adults of susceptible age and weak wills," especially "romantic and foolish girls of this latter type."

CLAP FOR THE WOLFMAN
Horror films didn't fare too well, either. The 1931 classic *Dracula*, starring Bela Lugosi, was banned because of its "unwholesome and gruesome effect." *The Ape Man* (1943) was rejected because "this is a horror picture and extremely frightening, and…we have decided to reject all horror pictures for the duration of the war [i.e., World War II]."

MUSTN'T OFFEND GOD

Movies were banned for religious reasons, as well. Cecil B. DeMille's romance *The Woman God Forgot* (1917) was prohibited simply because of its title. (After all, God doesn't forget anybody.) *Rain* (1932) was forbidden because it was "subversive to the teaching of the Founder of Christianity" and was "not conducive to [the] Christian belief in [the] power of divinity to keep [people] from sin." It also contained an "objectionable repetition of sacred prayers and phrases" and "the profane exclamations of a soldier" and it exalted "human romance as the only reality versus Christian belief."

POLITICS AND AUTHORITY FIGURES

International politics and the questioning of authority could cause a movie to be banned. *Adventure in Sahara* (1938) was rejected for both reasons. The censor described it as a "slanderous portrayal of conditions existing in the French Foreign Legion." Furthermore, "we feel that authority at the present time is being challenged at every opportunity, and if this picture was permitted to be shown in our public theatres, unquestionably it would be used as a case against constituted law and authority." *Outrages of the Orient* (1948), a docudrama about Japanese atrocities during World War II, was banned in 1952 because "in the light of present day events and a world trying to rise above feelings of hatred and revenge, I consider the showing of this picture to be against the public welfare."

NO TO MICKEY MOUSE

Even Walt Disney's animated cartoons *Mickey's Follies* and *The Skeleton Dance* (both 1929) were rejected—the former because of "vulgarity" and the latter because it was "gruesome."

Ceasing Censorship

In 1931, British Columbia's movie censor rejected 74 movies, more than in any other year, but by the 1950s and '60s only one or two films on average were banned annually.

Not Banned, but Get the Scissors Out

Because of their ability to keep films out of BC's movie theatres, censors could demand that cuts be made before a flick could be seen in the province. For example, all references to the Prince of Wales and the King of England had to be removed before the Marx Brothers' 1929 comedy *Cocoanuts* was permitted in local cinemas. *Sunnyside Up* (1929) couldn't be shown until a scene with a birth control magazine was deleted. *She Couldn't Say No* (1930) was not permitted in BC until the few seconds showing a girl thumbing her nose was cut nor was 1932's *Hell Fire Austin* allowed in the province until its name was changed to *Dare Devil Austin*.

Other movies that ran afoul of BC's movie censor include the famous 1930 anti-war film *All Quiet on the Western Front,* the Japanese classic *Rashomon* (1950), the multiple Academy Award winner *From Here to Eternity* (1953), Marlon Brando's breakout film, *The Wild One* (1953) and Bridget Bardot's famous *And God Created Woman* (1956).

In case you're wondering—Chaplin's *His Night Out* was given the axe because it contained a "burlesque of a minister." And *Abbott and Costello Meet Frankenstein* was banned because it was "nothing more than a reproduction in most part of the horror pictures *Frankenstein* and *Dracula* and as horror pictures are being banned from showing [as they had been since World War II], this is classified as such." The Appeal Board sustained this latter rejection.

CASE FILE
I Like It, but the Public Won't

While BC's movie censor liked the photography in
Black Narcissus in 1947, he pointed out that the
law required him to prohibit movies that would offend
"any body of people or may be likely to offend the
public." With that in mind, the censor felt that "the
characters in the film and the attitudes displayed…cre-
ate an impression that constitutes an affront to religion
and religious life" and, therefore, the movie was not going
to be seen. (The Appeal Board later overruled him.)

But I Saw the Movie in Ottawa!

Just because a movie was banned in British Columbia
didn't mean that it couldn't be seen elsewhere in Canada.
For example, the 1942 Russian war film *Diary of a Nazi* was
banned from BC theatres in 1947 in part because the censor
felt "its general use today would be purely Russian propaganda
giving the greatest comfort and encouragement to
Communistic organizations." The censors in Ontario, however, had no such concerns and approved the movie.

Likewise, just because Canadians elsewhere couldn't see
a movie did not mean that British Columbians couldn't. For
instance, Ontario's censors banned *Pretty Baby* (1978) while
BC's allowed it.

Too Many American Flags

Canadian nationalism was on the rise in the 1910s, particularly once World War I started in 1914. However, it seemed

to many at the time that American flags were cropping up everywhere in the movies and newsreels while the Union Jack (the Maple Leaf was not yet our flag) was nowhere to be seen. One Canadian film executive complained about "American films depending entirely upon vain glorious flag waving for their 'punch.'" The public's irritation with all those Stars and Stripes grew worse after the United States entered World War I in 1917 and American films and news-reels about the fighting ignored Canada's and other allied contributions to the war effort. Since BC's Moving Pictures Act required the censor to examine and determine the suit-ability of all films "with a view to the prevention of the depiction of scenes…which may be likely to offend the pub-lic," American flag-waving became the third most common reason (behind seduction and infidelity) for a movie to be banned or cut in British Columbia.

The Censor May Like It, but I Don't

BC's film censor wasn't the only person who could stop the public from seeing a movie. For instance, the Japanese drama *In the Realm of the Senses* (1976) came to Vancouver in 1978. Although it contained explicit scenes of sex and mutila-tion, the BC film censor didn't object to it. (Neither did the Québec censor, but the film was banned throughout the rest of Canada.) After the movie opened at the Varsity Theatre's Festival of International Films, the city's senior Crown Counsel, Richard Israels, and five police officers showed up for a private screening. Israels announced the following day that showing the film would violate the obscenity provisions in the federal Criminal Code. Section 159 (8) of the code outlawed any book, magazine, film or other media "with a dominant characteristic of which is the undue exploitation of sex, or of sex and any one or more of the following subjects, namely crime, horror, cruelty and violence."

Other provisions of Section 159 made illegal the exhibition on film of foul language, full frontal nudity and the simulation of intercourse and other sex acts.

Faced with the threat of criminal charges and fines, and the anticipated financial costs of defending itself in court (even if it won an acquittal), Varsity Theatre quickly pulled the film.

Note: *In the Realm of the Senses* was shown at Vancouver's Pacific Cinematheque theatre in April 2011. No one raised any concerns about the movie then.

Warning

Rather than banning or demanding changes in films, BC's film censor started adding warning labels to movies in the mid-1960s. Among the labels were the following:

The Exorcist (1973): "Warning: A very frightening picture, some extremely coarse language."

Texas Chainsaw Massacre (1974): "Warning: An extremely gruesome, disgusting picture."

The Three Musketeers (1973): "Warning: Excessive swordplay."

ON STAGE

Your Play Needs an Okay

Under Section 36 (10) of Vancouver's Bylaw 2944 (adopted in 1946), the city's chief licence inspector had the power to cancel, suspend and revoke the business licence of any theatre that produced an "immoral or lewd theatrical or dramatic performance or exhibition of any kind." The bylaw also gave the inspector the "full power to prohibit or prevent any indecent or improper performance or exhibition."

And then there was Section 277(c) of the City Charter, which was adopted in 1953. That bylaw gave the inspector the right to summarily suspend anybody's business licence if, in his opinion, the holder of the licence was guilty of "such gross misconduct…as to warrant the suspension." The term "gross misconduct" was not defined anywhere in the charter, and a 1967 court decision (involving the suspension of the *Georgia Straight* newspaper's business licence) held that the term's meaning was left to "the sole opinion of the Chief License [sic] Inspector." As a result, if the chief licence inspector was a prude, Vancouver was a very unlikely place to present an off-Broadway play that involved the actors taking off their clothes.

Give Me a Head of Hair, Long, Beautiful Hair

The rock musical *Hair* opened off-Broadway in October 1967, and on Broadway itself six months later. Other productions soon began all across Canada, the United States and Europe, but not in Vancouver. You see, the two-act play includes a 30-second nude scene that's performed in semi-darkness, so when the Vancouver Playhouse announced its intention to put on the musical in May 1969, Milt Harrell, Vancouver's chief licence inspector, told the Playhouse's artistic director to think again.

As chief licence inspector, Harrell had the absolute right to say what could and could not be performed on stage in Vancouver. But while the Hair controversy was going on in the city, theatre audiences could see fully nude actors perform at Simon Fraser University in nearby Burnaby.

The Vancouver Playhouse, fearing the loss of its business licence, backed down and Hair was dropped. Hugh Pickett, a promoter who was about to lose a $35,000 non-refundable deposit if the play was not put on, offered Harrell a free trip to Los Angeles so he could see the musical himself, but the inspector declined. And on July 8, Harrell closed down The Gallimaufry's production of

Camera Obscura (a futuristic drama about female-male alienation) at the Arts Club, where the two actors wore revealing see-through plastic robes but did not touch each other.

The public reaction to Harrell's actions was so hostile that the Vancouver City Council repealed on July 15, after much heated debate, the "immoral and lewd" suspension provisions of Bylaw 2944. It did so, however, with full knowledge that Harrell could still ban any theatrical performances he wanted under the city charter's Section 277(c) "gross misconduct" clause. The repeal did not stop the controversy. Finally, on July 22, council directed Harrell not to use his powers under Section 277(c) to interfere with any theatrical production.

Hair had its Vancouver debut one year later.

Lone Voice

When Vancouver's city council voted in 1969 to repeal Bylaw 2944, there was only one vote against the action. Before casting his ballot, the lone dissenter, Alderman Ed Sweeney, stated, "I will not allow any change in the law which will permit permissiveness to degenerate our society… I may be square and not with it, but I think the people in [*Hair* and *Camera Obscura*] are morally degenerate."

Nobody Is Safe

Section 277(c) of the Vancouver City Charter, which gave Milt Harrell the power to suspend anybody's business licence if, in his opinion, there had been "such gross misconduct…as to warrant the suspension," is still in effect.

You Can't Do that on Stage!

Under Vancouver Bylaw 952, adopted in 1912, it was against the law for anyone to produce a "theatrical, dramatic or picture exhibition" that was "immoral or lewd" or that contained any "immoral, lewd, lascivious, blasphemous or obscene language." And it wasn't just the producer who could get in trouble with the law. According to the statute, performers were not to sing songs "of an immodest, blasphemous or immoral character" or appear in any shows "in which any person shall perform any lewd acts or movements or make any licentious gestures." Anyone who ignored the bylaw faced a hefty fine or even possible jail time.

There was nothing in the bylaw, however, to specify what would be considered blasphemous, immoral, lascivious, lewd, licentious or obscene.

Billy the Kid Meets Jean Harlow

Two weeks after the Vancouver City Council clipped Milt Harrell's wings, The Gallimaufry theatre company opened its production of *The Beard*. The play is a dramatization of an imaginary encounter between 19th-century outlaw Billy the Kid and 1930s sex goddess Jean Harlow. The performance contains a lot of sexually explicit language and one scene of simulated cunnilingus.

The Beard's great commercial success was a result, at least in part, of the publicity raised by the *Hair and Camera Obscura* controversies. The local authorities did not interfere during the production and, one year later, The Gallimaufry decided to put on *The Beard* again. This time, however, after allegedly receiving a complaint from some "unidentified" citizen, three plainclothes Vancouver police officers caught the show near the end of its two-week run. They did not like what they saw and, the following day, the two actors, the stage manager and the two owners of the Riverqueen (where the play was being held) were arrested for presenting an obscene performance in violation of the federal Criminal Code. The matter went to trial in 1971 and, despite a litany of expert and character witnesses (including an Anglican archbishop) who stressed that words and scenes could not be isolated from the context of the entire play, all were convicted. Their collective fines amounted to $1250.

The case was appealed, but County Court Judge Graham Ladner found that the dominant characteristic of *The Beard* was an undue exploitation of sex and upheld four of the five convictions. He did, however, suspend the fines. Despite the suspension, the four remaining defendants still had a criminal record, which meant that the two actors could never work in the United States. It also meant that one of the actors and one of the Riverqueen's proprietors, both of whom were not

Canadian citizens, faced the possibility of deportation. So the four appealed to a higher court.

The matter finally came to a close in 1973 when the BC Court of Appeal unanimously reversed the lower court decisions. Writing for his fellow judges, Chief Justice Nathan Nemetz held that *The Beard* and other stage performances should be viewed in light of contemporary social attitudes. "I would agree," he wrote, "that the last scene would offend many people. However, it is not the personal taste of a judge that determines whether a work is obscene or not."

No Vancouver-area theatre production has since been charged with obscenity.

Watch Out for Those Women

A 1907 Vancouver bylaw made it unlawful to "take part in any theatrical or dramatic exhibition in which women or girls shall perform any lewd acts or movements, or make any licentious gestures." Again, no guidance was provided as to what would be considered lewd or licentious.

The Watch Around the Ankle

Hair wasn't the first stage performance to run afoul of Vancouver's licence inspector. The same thing happened to Marie Lloyd during her North American tour in 1914.

Lloyd was an internationally famous British music hall performer and comedienne whose stage act was very controversial for her day. Among her specialties was to sing the most mundane and innocent of songs with just enough inflection in her voice, along with enough of a raised eyebrow and a smirk on her face, to make it seem that the tunes came straight out of the pages of a dirty novel. Her personal life was scandalous, too. For example, during her 1914 tour, Lloyd was nearly deported from the United States when American immigration officials discovered that she was travelling with a man who was not her husband, but a horse jockey who was 18 years her junior.

Lloyd came to Vancouver for a sold-out engagement at the old Orpheum Theatre. Mayor T.S. Baxter and city licence inspector Charley Jones were not pleased with her arrival, and Baxter sent Jones to attend one of the performances. Based on Jones' report, the mayor said that "two of Marie Lloyd's songs might go all right in London, but Vancouver would not stand for them."

Another account says Jones issued orders that "no less than three of Miss Marie Lloyd's songs must be eliminated from her performance" and that "there must be less suggestiveness interpreted into the [other] songs." One of the tunes in question was "The Ankle Watch" during which Lloyd would lift up her floor-length dress a few inches to expose a watch around her ankle (which was very risqué for the time). Lloyd refused to comply, and just before showtime on Saturday, February 7, 1914, the mayor ordered Lloyd not to go on stage.

Baxter had the power to do it. In 1914, it was just not a matter of the Orpheum losing its business licence; both Lloyd and the theatre's manager, James Pilling, could also have been issued severe fines or gone to jail.

Furthermore, Mayor Baxter would be Lloyd's judge, jury and executioner! Under Bylaw 952, he could sit as the presiding judge in Lloyd's and Pilling's trial and, upon their conviction, fine the pair up to $100 (that's over $2000 in today's money). If Lloyd and Pilling couldn't pay, then they faced up to two months in jail.

Lloyd went on stage at the Orpheum that Saturday night and tried to explain why she could not perform, but she broke down in tears. The audience prevailed upon Lloyd to join the cabaret matinee at the old Hotel Vancouver, where she was loudly applauded. Poor Mr. Pilling, however, had to issue refunds.

Tobacco Road

It wasn't nudity that got the cast of *Tobacco Road* in trouble in Vancouver on January 16, 1953.

The play was based on a novel that was written in 1932 by Erskine Caldwell. The theatrical version came to Broadway the following year, where it was performed more than 3000 times before director John Ford brought it to the screen in 1941.

Tobacco Road is about the experiences of poor white tenant farmer Jeeter Lester and his Augusta, Georgia, family during the Great Depression. The book, the play and the movie were all popular but controversial; the play was banned in England and in large segments of the United States, censors in Hollywood tried to prevent the film from being made, and the movie was not permitted in theatres in Australia.

The uproar over *Tobacco Road* was a result of the irreverent portrayal of the extreme religiosity of some of the characters, but that's not what got the Vancouver cast arrested on obscenity charges.

The play opened on January 7, 1953, at Vancouver's Avon Theatre and continued before sold-out crowds without incident for one week. Because of its content, advertising contained the warning "Adult Entertainment Only" and no one under 18 was permitted entrance. But at some point an "unnamed citizen" phoned in a "bitter" complaint about actor Doug Haskins who, in one scene, seemed to be peeing in a cornfield. Two plainclothes detectives (one male and one female) were sent to watch two performances and they declared the play "lewd and filthy." The cops particularly objected to some torrid love scenes, which they described as "very bad." City Prosecutor Gordon Scott ordered the theatre on January 15 to "clean up" the production (without specifying how) or arrests would be made. Theatre representatives met with Scott and Mayor Fred Hume, but to no avail.

On January 16, nine Vancouver police officers interrupted the show and hauled the five cast members off to jail amid boos, jeers, whistles, stomping of feet and shouts of "Gestapo" from the nearly 1000 people in the audience. The director, Dorothy Davies, who had herself been threatened with arrest by Scott for "offending public morality," calmed everyone down and got them back to their seats for an impromptu performance of piano music and storytelling. About two hours later, the five actors returned to the stage and finished their performance after they each posted $100 bail (which was five times the maximum fine).

The five were charged with putting on an indecent and immoral performance in violation of the federal Criminal Code. Charges were also later laid against Davis as well as theatre operator (i.e., publicity agent) Charles Nelson and the producer, Sydney Risk. If convicted, the actors faced up to three months in jail and a $20 fine (about $160 today). Davis, Nelson and Risk, because they were in charge, were liable for up to one year in jail and a $500 fine.

The trial judge stated on February 13 that the play "catered to the lower instincts of the vast majority of those in the audience and was therefore indecent, immoral and obscene." Davies and the five actors were sentenced to pay $20 or spend 10 days in jail. Nelson was fined $50 or 20 days in jail. Risk was acquitted on a technicality. A county court judge reversed the convictions on appeal, but the City Prosecutor appealed that decision as a "test case" against one of the actors, and the BC Court of Appeals reinstated the conviction.

IN PRINT

I Dare You to Arrest Me

William A. Pritchard, the future mayor of Burnaby, taunted the police to arrest him in a Victoria speech in 1919. He owned two copies of Karl Marx's *Das Kapital;* one published by a British publisher, George Allen, and the other by an American firm, Charles H. Kerr and Company of Chicago. The copies were literally identical; both were printed from plates that Kerr had purchased from Allen years before. But while it was okay for Pritchard to have the Allen copy, possession of the Kerr edition was illegal.

Charles H. Kerr and Company was the foremost publisher of Marxist books and other materials in the United States, some of which found their way into Canada. The company was also a strong opponent of World War I and urged people to "paralyze the industrial machinery that makes war possible." This call for action was not welcomed by the Canadian government, which had been fighting the war since 1914. So the federal government, in an Order-in-Council under the War Measures Act, banned the importation of everything that Kerr and Company produced, including all books, pamphlets, even postcards—and *Das Capital*. The mere possession of any Kerr-produced item could result in a five-year prison sentence.

Fuel for the Fire

Victoria mayor Claude Harrison announced in 1954 that he was in favour of book burning. He even offered the use of his own fireplace. "Any books or literature," Harrison said, "which are of a seditious or subversive nature will go out of the library as far as I'm concerned…And any member of the library staff who belongs to a Communist organization will go out behind the book…It's time that many libraries throughout Canada are cleaned up."

Not to be outdone, Social Credit MLA Lydia Arsons said "these books should be destroyed. If we remove all books about Communism and by Communists we are not denying any citizens freedom."

No Violent Comic Books

Kamloops' Member of Parliament E. Davie Fulton and Victoria's Eleanor Gray of the Parent-Teacher Council blamed crime comic books for criminal violence, juvenile delinquency and an assortment of other problems. They together pushed a private member's bill, the Fulton Comic Book Bill, through Parliament in 1949 that made it an offence under the federal Criminal Code to make, print,

publish, distribute or sell "any magazine, periodical or book which exclusively or substantially comprises matter depicting pictorially the commission of crimes, real or fictitious."
It was even illegal to own one! Among the banned comics were *Amazing Mysteries*, *Captain America*, *Gunsmoke*, *Mr. District Attorney* and *The Two-Gun Kid*.

Scott v. Tobacco Road

While City Prosecutor Gordon Scott was shutting down the Vancouver performance of *Tobacco Road* in 1953, he also succeeded in removing from local bookstores and newsstands the 1932 novel that the play was based on.

It was revealed in January 1953 that, shortly after the passage of the Fulton Comic Book Bill, the city's two book and magazine distributors went to Scott and asked that he advise them whenever he thought a publication should be removed from public view. Specifically, anytime Scott received a complaint about a book or a magazine, he would pass it on to the distributors along with his comments. It was a nonbinding arrangement and it was understood that Scott would not necessarily prosecute the distributors for obscenity under the federal Criminal Code if they did not comply with his opinion. The local police, and everyone else, were completely unaware of the deal.

As described by Scott, "I have a very definite understanding with the distributors that my opinion shouldn't weigh. I read the books merely to see if I should pass on the complaint." Furthermore, *Tobacco Road* was just "one of quite a number of publications that we have suggested be taken off the shelf." A spokesman for Vancouver Magazine Service Ltd., the local distributor for *Tobacco Road*, commented that "we don't want anything to do with this trouble. These books are a very small part of our total business."

No Canadian History Here!

Stephen Leacock, one of our country's greatest and most prolific writers, authored a work entitled *Canada: The Foundations of Its Future* in 1941. It was a history book. And it was banned in British Columbia in 1959.

BC's Liquor Act prohibited all alcohol advertising in the province. Leacock's book was not only paid for and printed by a liquor company, the House of Seagrams, but the sponsorship was prominently displayed on its front cover. Forget about what was written between the covers; as far as the authorities were concerned, the text was nothing but an advertisement for alcohol and had to go.

No Articles on Wine Tasting, Either

The Labour Day issue of the *Vancouver Sun* was banned from the BC ferry *Queen of Burnaby* in 1971. Why? Because ferry workers on the ship noticed that it contained an article on Canadian wine tasting. And there was also that Bank of Montreal ad that showed a bottle of champagne being smashed against the wall of a new bank branch. A brand-new

BC law forbidding liquor ads was just days old and the workers felt the paper violated the statute, but the issue was not pulled from other ferries or from any other newsstands across the province.

Extra! Extra!

There were a lot of complaints in the Fraser Valley in 1994 about the free gay-lesbian newspaper *Xtra! West*. Some objected to its sexually explicit personal ads and others believed the paper would "corrupt" their youth.

On November 23, 1994, the board of the Fraser Valley Regional Library, whose 22 branches serve communities from White Rock to Hope, voted to allow local municipal councils to ban any free publications from their local libraries that the councils believed violated their "community standards." Abbotsford, Langley, Maple Ridge and Mission quickly barred *Xtra! West* from their library shelves; Maple Ridge's mayor, Carl Durksen, even removed the copies himself.

Of course, lawyers have to muck things up, and the Fraser Valley Regional Library Board was soon told that their action violated the Charter of Rights and Freedoms. So the board decided on February 8, 1995, to allow their branches to ban every free publication that contained paid advertising. It was an all or nothing deal; they could not single out *Xtra! West* and leave the rest alone. The next thing you knew, over 40 magazines and newspapers suddenly found themselves no longer welcomed at libraries across the Fraser Valley, including the *Abbotsford Times*, *BC Book World*, *Block Parent*, *The Children's Reader*, *The Christian Info News*, *The Computer Player*, the *Georgia Straight*, *Independent Senior* and the *Langley Times*.

The public response was quick, hostile and intense, so the board rescinded its decision one month later. *Xtra! West* and the other publications were returned to the libraries, but now any issue of any newspaper or magazine that has "excessive sexual content" is to be placed behind the library's counter or stored on a shelf at least 1.75 metres above from the library's floor.

The *Georgia Straight*

A FILTHY RAG

The first issue of Vancouver's alternative "underground" counterculture newspaper, the *Georgia Straight*, came out on May 5, 1967. That issue was 12 pages long and cost only a dime. It included articles about the youth movement in Amsterdam, a police raid at Vancouver's Douglas Gallery where a painting was seized and the gallery's owner was arrested for obscenity, and a reprint of a San Francisco piece about drug and other problems in Haight-Ashbury.

Tame stuff by today's standards, but the newspaper's contents were enough to get the attention of the local authorities. One week later, the same day the paper moved out of the apartment of its founder, Dan McLeod, into an actual office, McLeod was arrested by the police, taken away in a paddy wagon and jailed for three hours for "investigation of vagrancy." However, no charges were ever filed.

YOU'RE OUT OF BUSINESS!

On September 28, 1967, six weeks after the *Georgia Straight* received its business licence, Vancouver's chief licence inspector, Milt Harrell, advised the paper that the licence had been suspended and that he would recommend its permanent cancellation to the city council. The suspension came without any prior warning and cited no reasons for Harrell's action. The notice did say, however, that Harrell was acting in accordance with Section 277(c) of the City Charter, which gave Harrell the right to summarily suspend anybody for "gross misconduct."

The next day, Mayor Thomas Campbell stated in a television interview that it was he who suggested to Harrell that the *Georgia Straight*'s licence be cancelled. "As far as I'm concerned, this was a 'rag' paper; it was a dirty paper; it was being sold to our school children; and I wouldn't tolerate it on the streets any longer."

The *Straight* immediately went to court for a preliminary injunction to stop the city from suspending its licence. The judge said no. According to Mr. Justice Dohm, the statute left it up to the chief licence inspector to decide what constitutes "gross misconduct." The judge even praised Mayor Campbell and Inspector Harrell for the "suspension of this 'newspaper' and thus preventing the distribution of this filth." So much for the court upholding free speech and the freedom of the press.

Harrell reinstated the *Georgia Straight*'s licence at the end of October. In a letter, he stated that "in view of the contents of the most recent issue of the *Georgia Straight*, which I have examined, the suspension of your publisher's licence is no longer in effect." In other words, as long as the contents of the *Straight* did not offend Milt Harrell, the newspaper could stay in business.

ARREST ME! ARREST ME!
The New Westminster City Council denied the *Georgia Straight* a business licence in March 1968. The *Straight*'s editor, Dan McLeod, personally challenged the ban by selling issues on New West's streets in the hope of getting arrested. (He argued that the freedom of the press and the Canadian Bill of Rights, the predecessor to the Charter of Rights and Freedoms, guaranteed the *Straight* the right, licence or no, to sell papers.) McLeod was confronted by a cop, but he wasn't busted.

The New West council then passed a bylaw prohibiting the sale of literature on its city streets. The *Straight*'s vendors got around this by handing out copies for free and asking for a donation.

Then the New Westminster City Council passed Bylaw 4339 in September 1968. This new bylaw made it illegal for anyone, except the Jehovah's Witnesses, to sell or distribute for free any publication on the city's streets and sidewalks. However, because newspapers like the *Province*, the *Vancouver Sun* and New West's *Columbian* continued to be sold by vendors without any incident, the British Columbia Civil Liberties Association (BCCLA) concluded that the bylaw was aimed specifically at the *Straight*. So, on September 6, the BCCLA challenged the constitutionality of the ban.

Members of the association handed out the *Straight* on the streets of New Westminster that day in the hope that they'd be arrested. Unfortunately, no constables showed up and no arrests were made. BCCLA member Brian Carpendale lost his patience after one hour and filed a citizen's complaint against BCCLA president John Stanton for distributing the *Straight* in violation of the bylaw.

Nothing happened despite repeated requests from the BCCLA that the matter be promptly brought to court. Finally, after 10 days, City Prosecutor Morley Kalnitsky advised the association that he concluded Bylaw 4339 did not apply to newspapers and, therefore, no action was going to be taken against Stanton or any future *Straight* vendors.

WHERE ELSE?
Other than Vancouver and New Westminster, the *Georgia Straight* was also banned in 1967 and '68 in Haney, North Vancouver, West Vancouver, Squamish, Surrey and White Rock.

WELCOME TO THE 21st CENTURY

New Westminster banned the *Georgia Straight* again in 2007 by passing a bylaw that prohibited from the city's downtown core any news boxes that carried free newspapers. The move affected 20 boxes carrying the *Straight*, but it did not affect the boxes of newspapers for which people had to pay to get a copy, like the *Province* and the *Vancouver Sun*.

The city claimed that there was a growing litter problem. It also pointed out that free newspapers were still available in boxes at New West's two SkyTrain stations as well as various businesses that were located on private property.

The *Straight* said, however, that it serviced its boxes every week, a mess had never been found, and that other munici-palities, unlike New West, always contacted the *Straight* whenever there was a concern about littering. One critic of the ban (a local MP) also said that the "chain freebies," not the independent papers like the *Straight*, caused the litter problem.

You Can't Bring that into BC!

The vast majority of books, magazines and other publications found in BC's libraries and stores are not printed or published in Canada, but in the United States. But from whatever country they originate, all imported printed materials are subject to seizure by the Canada Border Services Agency (formerly Canada Customs).

An 1867 federal statute (i.e., An Act Imposing Duties of Customs) authorized Ottawa to ban and seize all foreign "books and drawings of an immoral or indecent character." However, the law contained no definition or guidelines as to what "immoral" or "indecent" meant. The law stood for over 100 years until the Federal Court of Appeal held in 1985 that the phrase "immoral or indecent" was an overly vague restriction on the freedom of expression found in the Charter of Rights and Freedoms. Parliament has since approved a definition of what is obscene and, thus, subject to seizure.

There was no right under the law until 1958 to go to court and appeal the ban of a publication; before then, all an importer could do was to plead his case before the Tariff Board (which refused to hear any appeals until, coincidentally, 1958 when it overturned the ban of Grace Metalious' *Peyton Place*).

Furthermore, the government once made public a list of what was banned, but stopped the practice in 1958. Even today, the titles of the books, magazines and other printed items that are prevented from importation are an official government secret.

While federal in scope, this censorship law has had some interesting results in British Columbia.

What Book Does the Professor Want Me to Read?

For years, the students in the modern literature course at the University of British Columbia found a blank space in their reading list. Those "in the know" knew that the empty line referred to one of the greatest literary works of the 20th century, *Ulysses* by James Joyce. (Although copies were on the shelf at the UBC library, they were illegal!)

Ulysses was banned from importation into Canada on January 26, 1923. No reason was given, but the work, which had been published in sections in American and British magazines between 1914 and 1921 and as a single book in 1922, was already forbidden in the UK and the U.S. for its sexual frankness.

The American and British bans were lifted in the 1930s, but it was still against the law to bring a copy of *Ulysses* into Canada. That is, until David Sim, the Deputy Minister of Customs and Excise (the Department of National Revenue was then in charge of imports), was casually reminded of the prohibition in 1949. He took *Ulysses* with him on vacation (it is unknown if his was an illegally imported copy), read it and decided that the book was no longer obscene. The ban was quietly pulled that fall without any public announcement. UBC didn't get the word until the following spring.

Lawbreakers at the Victoria Library

One copy of *Ulysses* was hidden for years in the vault of the Victoria Public Library while the book was banned. It somehow got across the border by accident and ended up in the library's collection, where it remained under lock and key.

When a Writ Is Wrong

The RCMP in BC have at their disposal a little-known warrant known as a "writ of assistance" that they can use as a tool in their investigations.

The same writ can be used over and over, from one case to another, and it enables the police to enter any building (public, private or commercial) so long as they are searching for specific objects named in the warrant.

As said by a Mountie spokesman, "it [the writ] saves us going through all the formalities of getting separate search warrants for individual premises while we are on these investigations."

We wouldn't want to make things too difficult for the cops.

CASE FILE
Raid on the Vancouver Public Library

On October 14, 1961, the headlines of the *Vancouver Sun* read, "RCMP Raiders Hunting French Sex Novel Here. Library, Stores Target of Drive." What the Mounties were looking for when they fell upon the Vancouver Public Library (VPL), Duthie's Books and Kaye Books was Henry Miller's *Tropic of Cancer.*

The book, published in 1934, was described by the *Sun* as a "sex-packed confession of Bohemian life in Paris between the [world] wars," and it constitutes, along with the *Tropic of Capricorn* (which the RCMP were also looking for in the 1961 raid), Miller's semi-autobiographical account of his years in France.

The importation of the *Tropic of Cancer* into Canada was prohibited in 1958. The book had also been banned in the United States, but the American ban was lifted in August 1961, and several copies had been brought into BC in the following months by tourists, British Columbians returning home from the states and American publishing houses that were fulfilling orders from BC bookstores and libraries that did not know the book was banned. (Remember, the list of banned books was by now a state secret. In fact, the raid on the VPL was the result of a phone call from a library employee asking Customs if the book was on the list of proscribed works.)

The Mounties seized one copy of the *Tropic of Cancer* at Duthie's, but there were none at the library because they were all checked out. The novel was very popular and "the public was howling to get its hands on the book" explained the VPL's assistant director. The library did agree to call in their three volumes and hand them over once they were returned. Kaye Books didn't have any copies to give the cops.

Can't Read that Magazine

RCMP and Canada Customs agents in Nanaimo and Victoria prevented copies of the Bachelor magazine from entering British Columbia in November 1961. The reason? The rag contained excerpts from the *Tropic of Cancer.*

Little Sister's

YOU CAN'T ALWAYS GET EVERYTHING YOU WANT
Vancouver's gay and lesbian bookstore, Little Sister's, unexpectedly found itself in Canada Custom's gun sights in 1986 when over 500 books and 77 magazines heading to its shelves for the Christmas season were seized at the border because some customs agents found them "disgusting" and obscene. Thus began a legal battle that would last for over a decade.

While the fight raged, thousands of books and magazine destined for Little Sister's were stopped by customs, including the following:

- *Salome* and *Teleny* by Oscar Wilde

- *Querelle* by Jean Genet

- *The Story of O* by Anne Desclos (aka Pauline Réage)

- *The Satanic Verses* by Salman Rushdie

- *Shroud of Shadow* by Gael Baudino

- *Belinda's Bouquet* by Leslea Newman and Michael Willhoite (a children's book)

- *Dancing on My Grave* by dancer Gelsey Kirkland's memoir

- *Dzelarhons: Mythology of the Northwest Coast* by Anne Cameron

A MERE CHANGE IN TITLE
One work shipped to Little Sister's and seized by Canada Customs was the gay safe sex manual, *Safestud* by Max Exander. Ironically, a shipment containing an earlier edition

of the book, then simply entitled *Stud*, was not stopped at the border.

OOOPS. SORRY.

In the first shipment to Little Sister's that was detained by Canada Customs in 1986 were copies of two issues of *The Advocate*, a Los Angeles–based gay political magazine. The reason for the seizure? Customs thought its advertisements were a little too suggestive. Little Sister's took Canada Customs to court, but just weeks before the trial in 1988, the government reversed its judgement; it decided that the ads weren't obscene and allowed future issues of the magazine into British Columbia. However, Little Sister's couldn't get back the copies that had been seized. Customs had already burned the entire shipment to a crisp.

A HELPING HAND

In 1994, the Crown's lawyers, representing Canada Customs, asked Joseph Avery, the attorney for Little Sister's, for copies of the books that he intended to use at trial as evidence. They wanted six copies of each. Of course, it was impossible for Little Sister's to comply with the request; the books were still banned, all shipments to the bookstore were still intensely scrutinized by customs and the titles that the Crown wanted were certain to be seized.

Solution? Celia Duthie, the owner of Duthie Books, agreed to get the books for Little Sister's. The Duthie chain carried many of the same titles that were being denied to its small competitor, but Canada Customs had never detained or seized any of its shipments. So Celia Duthie placed the necessary order. The invoice was briefly inspected by customs when the shipment arrived at the border. No one hid anything; the titles were clearly labelled on the documentation. The box containing the banned books was waved through, unopened and untouched. And the Crown got its copies.

MADE IN CANADA

Little Sister's published and sold copies of *Forbidden Passages* in 1995 to help pay for its legal fees. The book is an anthology of stories from 19 works whose entry into Canada was banned by customs. Unlike those 19, this book was legal for Little Sister's to sell. Why? Because it was domestically published (by Marginal Distribution of Peterborough, Ontario).

IN SPEECH

No Blasphemous Speech

One of Vancouver's first bylaws, adopted in 1886, provided that nobody could "make use of any profane swearing, obscene, blasphemous or grossly insulting language or be guilty of any other vice, immorality or indecency in the City of Vancouver."

Free speech advocates would not like this bylaw. No definition or guidance was given as to what constituted profane, obscene or insulting speech. The ban against blasphemy would certainly be unconstitutional. Nothing was said to indicate what other acts or deeds would be considered "vice, immorality or indecency." And you'd have to watch your tongue at home, too; the bylaw wasn't limited to things said or done in public.

Human
Rights

British Columbia welcomes all people and tries to treat everyone fairly and equally, regardless of their sex, race, physical challenges and political beliefs. But that was not always the case. In fact, you don't have to go far into history to find a BC that you may not recognize.

EUGENICS
Let's Sterilize Them!

Although never taken to the extreme that it was in Nazi Germany, eugenics was practiced by the British Columbia government for over 30 years.

There was strong interest across England and North America during the early 20th century to reduce the number of insane people and those who were described as "feeble-minded," "subnormal" and "unfit." This was a time when intelligence, or the lack thereof, was thought to be hereditary. Many people blamed unemployment, poverty, overcrowding and crime on "defective" individuals. Some objected to the costs of supporting these people, and others saw sterilization as one way to "improve" the circumstances faced by BC's families because birth control was not yet socially acceptable or legal. And there were those who viewed sterilization, coupled with more restrictive immigration laws, as a way to promote nationalism and racial supremacy. As Mary Ellen Smith, the province's first woman MLA, said of government-mandated sterilization in the Legislative Assembly: "If this were done, the English-speaking peoples would maintain their position of supremacy on which the peace and prosperity of the world depend."

BC's Sexual Sterilization Act became law in 1933. It gave the provincial government the authority to sterilize institutionalized mental patients as well as inmates of the Provincial Industrial Home for Girls (where girls under 16 were sent if they were convicted of a crime or were deemed vicious, incorrigible or beyond their parents' control). However, the power was supposed to be exercised only after a special "Board of Eugenics" examined the person in question. The board had to determine that the subject was likely, if released into society, to have children who themselves "by reason of inheritance" would have "a tendency to serious mental disease or mental deficiency." And the individual to be sterilized had to consent in writing; if that individual was incapable of giving it, then consent had to be obtained from the spouse or a parent or guardian.

The problem was that many people were sterilized under the law without anyone's consent, and a number were subjected to surgery for improper reasons. Some men went through the procedure simply because they could not support their families; others did so because they were sleeping around, had "violent" tendencies or were afraid they'd make their wives pregnant again. Women were also sterilized because they were promiscuous, had illegitimate children, were suffering from what is today called postpartum depression or were epileptic.

About 200 people were sterilized pursuant to the act, and although the number started to drop off after 1936, there were still three or four sterilizations per year as late as 1968.

Nine women who were sterilized without their consent were awarded a $450,000 court settlement in 2005.

What's the Hurry?

The Sexual Sterilization Act took effect on July 1, 1933. The law was declared a failure by the *Victoria Daily Times* the following January when no one had yet been sterilized. (Indeed, the first sterilization did not occur until 1935.)

Many people also complained that the legislation was too limited in its scope and wanted all "defective" people, and not just those who were institutionalized, to be sterilized. And others said that the law placed too much emphasis on the rights of the individual over those of society in general. (The last argument sounds a little familiar, doesn't it?)

SOVEREIGN IMMUNITY
You Can't Sue Me, I'm the Government!

Ever been abused, wrongfully arrested or have your rights trampled by the police? Have your property damaged or taken away without due process of law? Or maybe something terrible happened to you at the hands of the government, like Gary Hill who, as a troubled teen residing at BC's Woodlands School in New Westminster, was put into a straightjacket and gassed into unconsciousness before all of his were teeth removed in 1967 as punishment for biting a member of Woodland's staff.

Until recently, you could not sue the province unless the provincial government first gave you the okay to do so. You see, there is a legal doctrine known as sovereign immunity that is hundreds of years old. It evolved from two ideas: first, that "the King could do no wrong," and second, that the monarch's right to rule comes directly from God (i.e., the divine right of kings). In short, the doctrine states that you need the government's permission if you wish to sue it for something it has done or for something its agents did on the government's behalf or while working for the government.

That all changed with the enactment of the Court Proceedings Act of 1974. BC can now be held liable for wrongdoing just as if it were a person. (British Columbia was the last province in Canada to abolish sovereign immunity.) However, there is a catch. The BC Court of Appeals held in 2005 that the statute is not retroactive and the Crown is still immune for anything it did before August 1, 1974, the date the act took effect. So while other abuse victims from Woodlands can take the province to court (the place wasn't closed until 1996), Gary Hill and the more than one thousand others like him who were abused before that date are out of luck and will never receive a dime.

WOMEN ARE PEOPLE, TOO!

You Can't Practice Law in BC. You're a Woman!

Ontario passed a law in 1892 allowing women to become lawyers and, on February 2, 1897, Toronto's Clara Brett Martin became the first female attorney in the British Empire. BC's Mabel Penery French wanted to follow in Martin's footsteps.

French was, in 1905, the first woman to graduate (with honours no less!) from the law program at King's College in New Brunswick. However, she was not allowed to practice because, according to the New Brunswick Supreme Court, no female could be a "person" as that term was defined by the statute governing the province's legal profession. Public pressure arising from the court's decision led to the law being changed in 1907 to allow women to be lawyers in New Brunswick.

French moved to Vancouver in 1910 and quickly got a job with a law firm as a solicitor and clerk. She applied the following year for admission to the Law Society of British Columbia to become a barrister so she could appear in court on behalf of her clients.

On the face of it, there should have been no obstacles. The members of BC's Legislative Assembly were presumably a group of rather smart people who kept abreast of what was going on across the country. Shortly after Clara Brett Martin became a lawyer in Ontario, the BC legislature adopted the Legal Professions Act of 1897, which stated that the benchers of the Law Society "may call to the Bar and admit to practice as a Barrister in British Columbia: (a) Any person being a British subject of full age and good repute." (BC was still part of the British Empire and Canadians were merely British subjects living in Canada.) The law also provided for the admission of British subjects who, like French, were already called to the bar in other provinces. And the British Columbia Interpretation Act of 1897, also enacted after Martin became a lawyer, stated that "words importing the … masculine gender only shall include…females as well as males and the converse."

But when French applied to take the bar exam in 1911, the BC Law Society benchers, by a vote of four to two, concluded that "there was no authority under the terms of the statute [i.e., the Legal Professions Act] to enrol lady applicants for call or admission" and refused to let her take the test.

French sued, but the Law Society relied in its defence upon the earlier New Brunswick Supreme Court decision that French was not a "person" eligible for admission to the bar. The judge agreed. He ruled that the Legal Professions Act dealt with "a particular class of British subjects…viz.: male persons—adults" and that "the [British Columbia] Legislature had not in mind the contingency that women would invoke the provisions of the Act." (Like, who else would invoke the statute? And remember, Martin was admitted as a lawyer in Ontario just before the Legal Professions Act was adopted, a fact that BC's MLAs were likely aware of.)

French appealed, but the BC Court of Appeal unanimously ruled against her, too, and held that the British Columbia Interpretation Act did not apply to the Legal Professions Act. It somehow reached the conclusion that "the context of our Act [i.e., the Legal Professions Act] refers to a profession for men, and men alone" and that it was "conclusive that the word 'person' in our own Act [the Legal Professions Act] was not intended to include a woman."

The appellate court's decision was announced on January 9, 1912, but anyone who thought the matter was over was nuts. Evelyn Farris, a prominent social activist and wife of Vancouver's Crown counsel, John Wallace Farris, took up French's cause and began a massive campaign on her behalf. Within weeks, the press and the public were bearing down heavily on the government to reverse the decision. On February 24, BC Attorney General William Bowser (himself a strong opponent to women's rights) introduced a bill to allow women to study and practice law in British Columbia. It took only three days for the measure to pass the Legislative Assembly and receive royal assent. Mabel Penery French was called to the British Columbia bar on April 1, 1912.

French Had a Prominent Supporter

One of the two Law Society benchers who voted in favour of Mabel French's admission to the bar was Sir Charles Hibbert Tupper. At first glance, he would seem a rather conservative pro-establishment figure. A prominent Vancouver attorney, he was the son of Prime Minister Charles Tupper and a former federal Minister of Justice. But Charles Hibbert Tupper not only backed French's attempts to join the bar, he also helped Japanese Canadians in their fight against discrimination.

Sex Disqualification

In 1931, it had been almost four decades since Mary MacNeill became British Columbia's first woman doctor (1893) and nearly 20 years since Mabel Penery French took the oath as the province's first female lawyer. Women could also vote, sit on juries and hold political office. They were actively participating in the province's civil life in many other ways, too, such as serving in the civil service and entering other professions.

But someone, apparently, still objected to the women playing any role outside the home, so the BC Legislative Assembly adopted the Sex Disqualification (Removal) Act, which stated the following:

> *A person shall not be disqualified by sex or marriage from the exercise of any public function, or from being appointed to or holding any civil or judicial office or post, or from entering or assuming or carrying on any civil profession or vocation, or for admission to any incorporated company or society.*

For good measure, the statute was made retroactive to July 20, 1871, the day that British Columbia joined Confederation, but a clause was added that the law's retrospective application would not affect any prior BC court decision that discriminated against anyone because of their sex.

One Last Sexist Hurdle in the Courtroom

Although women could already practice law and serve as judges in British Columbia (Helen Gregory MacGill was appointed BC's first female judge in 1917), they were not allowed to sit on juries in the province until 1922! And as bizarre as that sounds, British Columbia was actually the first province inthe country to let women serve as jurors. (Besides Nova Scotia, no other province allowed women on juries until 1950.)

The Jury Act Amendment Act was adopted in 1922. Before then, only a "person" was allowed to sit on a jury in BC and, under the British common law, women were persons only "in the matter of pains and penalties, not in the matter of rights and privileges." (It wasn't until 1929 that the British Privy Council ruled that women were "persons" under the British North America Act of 1867.)

There was some concern when the act was introduced in the Legislative Assembly about women hearing or seeing "disgusting" things in trials for such crimes as murder and rape. The law, therefore, required local sheriffs, after they made their annual preliminary list of potential jurors every May, to notify by registered mail all the women on the list that they had 15 days to tell him of their unwillingness to serve. If a woman did so, her name would not be placed on the final list of potential jurors that came out in June.

No such opt-clause existed for potential male jurors. This led one MLA to complain that "this is not a case of equal rights for women. It is a case of giving them superior rights." The clause remained, however, until 1964.

I DON'T LIKE YOUR COLOUR, CREED OR CULTURE

But He's a Communist!

In 1949, World War II veteran Gordon Martin, who had both "excellent credentials and academic standing," sought admission to the BC Law Society. His request was denied. The reason? He was a member of the Communist Party. The Law Society required all of its members to be of good repute and, as far as they were concerned, being a Red meant that he wasn't. Martin appealed the decision to the British Columbia Supreme Court but lost. He then gave up his dreams of being a lawyer and set up a television repair business.

You Can't Swim Here!

For decades, British Columbians of black, Chinese or Japanese ethnicity had to show up on Tuesdays between 10:00 AM and noon if they wanted to swim at Vancouver's first indoor public pool, the Crystal Pool (which was located near the site where the Vancouver Aquatic Centre is today). Why? Because the pool was open the rest of the week only to Caucasians.

The restriction began in the 1920s when the pool was privately owned, and the Vancouver Parks Board continued the policy after the city acquired the property in 1940. Only after five years of public controversy and debate did the board finally throw out the rule in 1945 and open the pool to the entire public regardless of race, colour or creed.

I Don't Care if It Is Your Own Money!

Those upstarts! How dare the First Nations spend their own money to hire lawyers to try to get their land back!

Native bands in British Columbia have been pressing their land claims since the 1850s, but things really became heated when lawyers like John Murray McShane Clark and Arthur Eugene O'Meara got involved in the early 20th century and became prominent advocates for Indian title. Now there was a chance that the law might actually be used to help the First Nations get their land back, and both the British Columbia and federal governments would have none of that. What to do? Simple. Make it a crime for any member of the First Nations to pay a lawyer to work on their behalf.

Falsely claiming that BC's First Nations were being robbed by dishonest attorneys, Parliament passed a law in 1927 making it illegal for anybody (Native or non-Native), without the prior written consent of the federal Superintendent General of Indian Affairs, to receive or request any payment or donation from any member of the First Nations in order to raise money to pursue a lawsuit on behalf of a Native band.

In other words, without the superintendent's permission (which was not likely to be granted), Clark and O'Meara would be committing a crime if they ever took money from a Native client. Unless they found some non-Native financial backers, the two would have to work for free and pay all the court costs and other expenses out of their own pocket. Furthermore, anyone who raised money among the First Nations on Clark's and O'Meara's behalf would also be in violation of the law. The penalty was a $50 to $200 fine or up to two months in jail.

Don't Hire that Woman!

New Westminster restaurateur Cheng Yau was fined $20 (about $245 today) plus court costs in 1919. His crime? Employing a white woman as a waitress.

The BC Legislative Assembly added a section to the Municipal Act Amendment Act (isn't that a tongue twister) shortly before Yau's arrest. The new provision prohibited all Caucasian women from working in, and even visiting as customers, any "restaurant, laundry or place of business or amusement owned, kept or managed by any Chinese person." The only exception was a "public apartment," where the white woman could live if she were a "bona fide customer." Any Chinese Canadian business owner who violated this law faced up to $100 in fines and up to two months in jail if the fine wasn't paid. However, the women who were employed at or frequented these places faced no criminal penalty.

Diplomatic Pressure

Because of harsh criticism from the Chinese Benevolent Association and China's top diplomat in Vancouver, Yang Shu-Wen, the provision of the Municipal Act Amendment Act was repealed in 1923, but it was instantly replaced with the Women's and Girls' Protection Act.

The new statute deleted all previous references to the Chinese, but as noble as its title sounds, it actually broadened the provisions of the earlier measure. No "Indian" (i.e., First Nation) or Caucasian woman or girl could now "reside in or lodge in or work in or, except as a bona fide customer of a public apartment thereof only, frequent any restaurant, laundry or place of business or amusement" where, in the opinion of the head of the local municipal or provincial police, it was "in the interest of the morals of such women and girls" that they

CASE FILE
No Threats to Female Morality

The Women's and Girls' Protection Act was not repealed until 1968. In the meantime, no police chief ever thought the PNE (i.e, the Pacific National Exhibition) or any movie theatre or dance hall "or other place of business or amusement" adversely affected the morals of BC's females—at least not enough to try to use the law to keep the women away. No one, that is, except Vancouver Police Chief William W. Foster in 1936.

Foster wanted eight Chinese restaurants to fire their white waitresses. Some complied. Others were cited by the police and went to court, but the judge wanted the name of every woman whose morals were being jeopardized. (Those damn liberal, criminal-coddling judges!) Taking the hint, the defendants quickly fired their help, whose names the police had, and replaced them with others whose names the police did not. Case dismissed.

Frustrated, Foster turned to the city's licence department. After all, according to City Prosecutor Oscar Orr, if "the Licence Inspector [discovers]…'loose conduct,' such as a white waitress sitting down with a Chinese [the shameless hussy], no outward crime is being committed but the chances are that procuring *may* well be under way [emphasis added]…[and then] the power to cancel licences should be used by the Licence Inspector."

☞

At Foster's request, Inspector H.A. Urquhart cancelled the licences of three Chinese cafés in January 1937. The café owners tried, but failed, to get a court injunction to stop Urquhart from putting them out of business. They now had no choice but to fire their Caucasian help. Everyone else got the message and, by October, all Chinese restaurants in Foster's crosshairs discharged their white female staff.

That James Dunsmuir, What a Guy!

The BC Legislature Assembly adopted an amendment in 1890 to the Coal Mines Regulation Act that barred any Chinese Canadian from working underground at a coal mine. The law was supposedly adopted because the Chinese workers had a limited command of English and could not clearly understand instructions or read warning signs and rules. But there was also an element of racism; the Asians were willing to work for about half of what their white counterparts earned, and Caucasian miners resented that fact. And there was a bit of politics and business competition at play, too; coal magnate and future premier James Dunsmuir and his Union and Wellington Collieries employed Chinese Canadians as underground workers, and his opponents wanted some way to strike at him.

The new law initially had little effect, but criminal sanctions were added in 1897 to punish violations of the law. That's when Dunsmuir went to court. He and his lawyers went all the way to the British Privy Council (then the highest court of appeal in the Canadian legal system) and got a decision in 1899 that the amendment was unconstitutional. At first it seemed that the Privy Council had protected the Chinese coal miners from discrimination, but subsequent court cases significantly narrowed the application of the decision. And what did Dunsmuir do when he heard the news that he won the case? He docked the wages of his Chinese employees to pay his lawyers' fees.

No Gifts From You!

The potlatch is an important cultural event for most of the First Nations along BC's coast. It serves many purposes, including the affirmation of one's status in a community and the celebration of a marriage or the naming of children. And a major part of a potlatch is the distribution of gifts by the host (although property is sometimes destroyed at a potlatch, too). So what did the government do? Why, ban it, of course.

The potlatch was made illegal by Parliament in 1884. The first person to be arrested for violating the law was brought before Judge Matthew Begbie five years later, but Begbie threw out the charges because the word "potlatch" was not defined in the statute, so the law was unenforceable. Parliament rewrote the law in 1895 and this time it stuck. To participate in a potlatch was a crime until 1951.

No Dancing! And Take Off Those Clothes!

Parliament enacted a law in 1914 that prohibited any member of BC's First Nations (as well as those in Alberta, Manitoba and Saskatchewan) from participating in any "Indian dance" outside their own reserve without the permission of the federal Superintendent General of Indian Affairs. Nor could a Native participate in any show, exhibition, performance, stampede or pageant while wearing an "aboriginal costume" without the Superintendent's okay.

So much for pow-wows, rodeos and Buffalo Bill's Wild West Show.

Proper
Public Attire
(or Lack Thereof)

You are not supposed to be ashamed of your body, but that doesn't mean everyone wants to see it, either. How much skin you can show, and under what conditions, has changed with the times, and so has the law that governs public displays of immodesty.

NAKED AS A JAYBIRD

A Prison for Nudists

Marching and demonstrating in the nude were tactics often used in the early 20th century by the Sons of Freedom, a radical sect of the Doukhobors, to protest laws that compelled their children to attend BC's public schools. Things got so bad that, in 1931, Parliament amended the federal Criminal Code to lengthen the maximum penalty for public nudity from six months to three years. Nearly 600 Doukhobor men and women were arrested the following year when they protested, sans clothing, along the highway between Castlegar and Nelson. All were convicted and given the maximum penalty. In fact, a special prison was established on Piers Island near Saanich just for them.

CASE FILE
It's My Body, and I'll Bare if I Want To

Linda Meyer frequently provoked authorities and went to jail in the 1990s for the right to go topless in public. In response to Meyer's statements that she intended to bathe top-free at the Leisure Centre Pool, the Maple Ridge City Council amended its bylaws on June 24, 1997, to require that all "females over the age of eight (8) years shall fully cover all portions of their nipples and aureole with opaque apparel." Meyer arrived bare-breasted at the swimming pool on July 1, refused requests to comply with the new bylaw and was given a ticket.

A court case in Ontario (*R. v. Jacob*) determined the previous year that appearing nude or semi-nude in public, in and of itself, was no longer an offence under the federal Criminal Code. Specifically, going topless was a crime only if a reasonable bystander, fully apprised of all the circumstances, believed that a woman was exposing her breasts for her own or someone else's sexual gratification.

When Meyer's case reached the BC Supreme Court, Justice R. R. Holmes ruled:

> *I do not find in the evidence support for the view that the parks could not operate in orderly fashion if a female were to bare her breasts in a circumstance that did not offend criminal laws of nudity. The evidence suggests the Section 3A amendment to the Park By-Law was more a reaction to a frustration that the criminal law [i.e., the Criminal Code] was not supporting the moral standards...that some Maple Ridge citizens desired.*

Therefore, Meyer threw out Maple Ridge's new bylaw.

No Nudists at Our Pools

For those who came of age in the 1960s, skinny-dipping would hardly seem to be a threat to the moral fibre of Western civilization. Not so, however, for some of the good burghers of Surrey.

So began BC Supreme Court Justice Williamson's decision in *Skinnydipper Services Inc. v. City of Surrey* (2007).

You see, the Federation of Canadian Naturists rented Surrey's Newton Wave Pool for private skinny-dipping once a month throughout 2002 and early 2003. The swims took place late in the evening, and only members of the group were permitted to attend. Furthermore, the pool's windows, which would have permitted members of the public to watch, were covered with an opaque material whenever the nudists were present.

Everything was going great until a newspaper article about the federation's swim was published. The pool's staff suddenly cancelled the group's pool rental permits. Shortly afterward, on March 31, 2003, the federation received a letter from the City of Surrey supporting the action. (The city council, by the way, decided to back the ban in a meeting that was closed to the public. How democratic.)

Surrey claimed that the permits were cancelled pursuant to a municipal bylaw it adopted in 1998. The regulation stated that "no person shall enter or bathe in any water at any bathing beach or in any swimming pool without being clothed in proper bathing attire."

The city argued that the bylaw was needed to bring Surrey into compliance with a provincial regulation concerning bathing attire. After all, requiring swimsuits to be clean when worn at public pools also meant that they, indeed, had to be worn. But Justice Williamson rejected the idea. He held that the provincial regulation dealt with public health and that no evidence had been brought to him that there was any health risk when people swam naked.

Williamson also found that the anti-nudity provisions of the federal Criminal Code apply only when nudists strut their stuff in a way the public can see. "Nudity is defined by Parliament. The offence in the code does not apply to persons who are on private property and not exposed to public view." Because no municipal council can expand the definition of a crime to include what is otherwise excluded by Parliament, Williamson found the Surrey bylaw to be unconstitutional.

In the Nude, in the Nude...

According to a portion of a 1905 public morals law, Kelowna once permitted nude bathing "in any public waters," but only between 9:00 PM and 6 AM. During peak hours, you had to wear a little more than just your birthday suit or face a fine of up to $100 (over $2300 today). The entire public morals bylaw was repealed in 1990, but dare to bare your nude body on one of Kelowna's public beaches today and you might still find yourself in hot water with the local officials.

MODEST SWIMMING APPAREL REQUIRED

Restrictions on Swimming Attire

An 1892 Vancouver bylaw required everyone who swam or bathed between 6:00 AM and 8:00 PM in those parts of Burrard Inlet or English Bay that were within the city limits to wear a bathing suit that covered the body from the neck to the knees. (The regulation was later amended to include False Creek.) There was no requirement regarding attire, however, for those who enjoyed the water between 8:00 PM and 6:00 AM. And the bylaw stayed on the books, unaltered, until 1986!

The Vancouver Park Board adopted a similar restriction in 1906. Their bylaw required everyone who swam or bathed in any waters under its care, including beaches and public pools, to wear a two-piece bathing suit (one-piece was okay if you were under 15) that covered everything from the shoulders to the knees.

Unlike the Vancouver City Council, the Park Board caught up with the times in 1933. The police were finding it difficult, in view of changing styles, to regulate the bathing costumes that people were wearing without arresting everyone. The Park Board first appointed a committee to study the issue and, in the meantime, left it to police discretion to "exercise control over persons appearing in costumes not considered modest." A few weeks later, the Board adopted a new bylaw that no one could wear a swimsuit that was "to any extent transparent" or "not entirely modest in make or style."

Damn Tan Lines

Forget about rolling down those trunks or sliding the straps of your bikini top off your shoulders to get a little extra sun. The Vancouver Parks Board 1933 bylaw made it illegal for "any person wearing a bathing suit to lower or roll down such suit while on a public bathing beach."

Skimpy Male Swim Trunks

Apparently people were particularly concerned about male swim attire in 1933. While the Vancouver Parks Board had nothing further to say about women's beach attire beyond that it could not be transparent or immodest, it was decreed that men's trunks had to be "of sufficient height to cover the navel with a three inch [7.5 centimetres] of leg square-cut."

No Sun Baths Here!

Forget about going in your swimsuit to Vancouver's Queen Elizabeth Park to throw a Frisbee or to sprawl out on a blanket and soak up some sun. The city's park board in 1933 decided that no one wearing swimwear could "loiter or play or indulge in sun baths in any public park or place, other than a bathing beach, or on the grass plots and picnic grounds of parks immediately contiguous to a bathing beach."

Crime

Fighting crime is serious business, but what one has to do to get the job done can sometimes be strange, odd or even humorous.

NOT ONLY CRIMINALS END UP IN JAIL

We Can Force You to Talk!

Back in 1968, Section 603 of the *Criminal Code of Canada* gave the courts the power to arrest anyone who was likely to give material evidence in a criminal case if it appeared that the individual would not voluntarily come to the trial to testify.

CASE FILE
I Promise to Come Back

The Section 603 provision had some rather unfortunate consequences for Vancouverite Joseph Fréchette.

On March 13, 1968, Réal Deslodges was murdered in Vancouver's skid row, and Frechette was taken into custody as a material witness. The judge thought Fréchette would be a no-show at trial, so two days later a warrant was issued for Fréchette's formal arrest. His bail was set at $500. Fréchette didn't have the money, so he stayed in jail until a preliminary hearing was held on May 8 for Briercliffe and Kazersky, the two men accused of killing Deslodges. The judge still thought that Fréchette wouldn't show up, and bail was again set at $500. Unfortunately for Fréchette, charges against one of the defendants were dropped, but new charges were quickly filed. The preliminary hearing for those new charges was on June 21, and another material witness warrant was issued for Fréchette (who, by the way, was still in custody on the first warrant). His bail was set at another $500. So now Fréchette needed $1000 to get out of jail.

Fréchette was finally released on his own recognizance in July after sitting in a cell for four-and-a-half months, but only after the British Columbia Civil Liberties Association got involved and provided him with a lawyer, free of charge.

In the hearing to decide whether Fréchette should be let go, Magistrate Jack Anderson initially said, "I fail to understand why this man has been unable to fulfill what I feel to be a most lenient bail requirement." Apparently Anderson had forgotten where Fréchette was picked up for questioning, but once Fréchette's financial situation was explained to him, Anderson changed his tune. "I am concerned about him having suffered unduly for having witnessed a murder with which he apparently had no connection."

Perhaps Fréchette found some consolation in the fact that the accused couldn't make bail either and were also sitting in a cell awaiting trial. Whatever satisfaction he got, however, was surely lessened by the fact that,

on October 23, at the recommendation of the
Crown, a stay of proceedings was issued and
the charges against Briercliffe and Kazersky were
dropped. As Magistrate A. Brown said when he
granted the stay, the court was "not constituted to
solve mysteries in fact insolvable by reason of an alcoholic
atmosphere and some very obviously unreliable witnesses." Too bad no one came to this realization *before*
Fréchette spent all those months in jail.

Victoria's Bobbies

Victoria had only 14 officers in 1881; that's one police officer
for every 423 residents! Furthermore, officers had only seven
pistols, eight batons and seven pairs of handcuffs between
them. By 1891, the number of police in the provincial capitol
had dropped to one officer for every 731 residents.

Surrey's Mighty Police Force
Surrey was incorporated in 1879, but the city council
didn't get around to hiring its first municipal police officer
until 1887 (and didn't bother to buy him a gun or a pair of
handcuffs until the year after that). It wasn't until there was
a murder in 1908 that Surrey built its first jail. (Until then,
Surrey's prisoners were held at the provincial prison
in New Westminster.)

West Van Cops
West Vancouver appointed its first constable in 1912.
However, the municipality had no police cars, so for years
anytime officers were called to perform their duty west of the
city core, they had to take a bus to get there.

SMUGGLING

Porous Border

Smuggling and illegal entry has always been a problem along the Canada–U.S. border near Surrey and White Rock. One of the more humorous episodes occurred in 1914 when three chaps pumped a handcar along the old New Westminster–Southern Railway track from Cloverdale to within a few metres of the international line. They then crossed the border, walked into Blaine, Washington, and loaded up a wagon with flour, apples and sugar. Back into BC they went, where they transferred their supplies to the handcar before returning to Cloverdale. Ironically, a Surrey police officer just happened to be in Blaine that same day and noticed what the lads were doing. The cop had his suspicions, crossed the border as soon as he could and rushed to Cloverdale (in a hired buggy, no less!) just in time to arrest the men and seize the goods.

WHERE CAN I ROLL SOME DICE?

Gambling Fines

Although gambling was illegal, Vancouver's Chinese community operated clubs, betting houses and gambling halls. Women were prohibited from the gambling dens (to cut down on prostitution), and the establishments were not tolerated outside Chinatown. These gambling houses were substantial cash cows for the city from about 1910 to the early '30s. The fines and forfeited bail paid by the gambling operators were just a part of their cost of doing business, and these entrepreneurs often paid the bail or fines of their customers as well. (The city jail didn't have enough room or resources for the hundreds of gamblers arrested anyway. Over 600 were busted in 1916 alone and the number climbed to nearly 4000 by 1925.)

There was a quid pro quo between the owners of these establishments and the police. The cops usually kept the number of raids and arrests to a minimum, and the local courts and bobbies frequently returned the money and equipment seized in raids whenever the accused pleaded guilty. In exchange, not only did gambling bring the city a lot of money in fines, but there was also an informal agreement that the police themselves would have easy access to the activity.

The Monte Carlo of Canada

Gambling was once so rampant in Sandon (now a ghost town about 10 kilometres east of New Denver) that it was known as the "Monte Carlo of Canada." Poker tables, slot machines and roulette wheels operated 24/7 in the city's plentiful gambling halls and other establishments, and many a fortune was won and lost. Gambling tables were even set up outside and doing business in the open air only one day after a devastating fire destroyed most of Sandon in 1900.

But when Sandon began to rebuild, the city council decided to clean up the downtown core and create a new image for the community, so it outlawed all forms of gaming.

On October 13, 1900, the headline in Sandon's *Paystreak* newspaper read, "Gambling Shut Down and Knights of the Green Cloth are on the Hike."

The "knights" were the professional card dealers and others who made their living from gambling. And the article underneath the headline lamented:

> *No more the little stacks of reds and blues pass back and forth at the behest of the fickle goddess of fortune. No more the roulette wheel burr nor the faro king reigns where dead games sports be'em to the rafters and lucky ikes double shoot the turn.... It's all off now. Chips that pass in the night are valuable only as souvenirs, and the agitation for the free and unlimited coinage of poker checks is only a matter of ancient history.*

House
and Home

*Provincial statutes and municipal bylaws have long
governed the construction and appearance of residences
and other buildings. But that's not all
they've regulated...*

BUILDING CODES

A Bit of the Alpines in BC

Located in the mountains, Smithers officially adopted an "alpine theme" in 1972 to give itself a more memorable appearance. To promote the look, all new structures in the downtown core must be built in the alpine, or *bauernhaus,* style, which includes peaked roofs, facades and deep overhangs.

Sorry, No Mail Today

The fire chief of Fernie, along with a detachment of other fire fighters and some police, began to tear down the city's post office on December 14, 1909.

A municipal bylaw required all temporary buildings within the city's limits to be removed by November 1. The post office was located in a temporary wooden structure and the postmaster, H.J. Johnson, had been given several warnings to move, but he didn't, so the city council ordered the building to be taken down. The new brick structure that was meant to be the post office's new home was not yet completed, and Johnson cried foul because the council had allowed other temporary structures within the fire limits to remain standing while their permanent replacements were built. As a result of the controversy, Fernie's mail service was briefly disrupted.

No Skyscrapers

The Vancouver City Council rejected in 1929 a proposal to increase the maximum height for buildings beyond the 10 storeys or 120 feet (36.5 metres) already permitted.

You're Obstructing My Light!

There is an old English legal concept that came to BC known as "ancient lights." The idea is that if you own a building with windows, and those windows have received natural sunlight for at least 20 years, you can forbid your neighbour and everybody else from doing anything, such as constructing another building or planting a tree, that will obstruct the sunlight.

The doctrine is great if you live in a small rural community where there aren't that many people around, but it's a nuisance (or worse) in an urban centre with skyscrapers, apartment buildings and other tall structures standing next to each other. So the Legislative Assembly abolished the doctrine in 1906. You can now rely upon the bylaw only if a previous owner of your building had acquired, before the 1906 legislation, the right to the uninterrupted access and use of sunlight.

KEEP THY NEIGHBOUR OUT OF THY SIGHT

A Crime to be Homeless

An 1892 Vancouver bylaw stated, "all vagrants and mendicants and persons without any visible means of support, within the said City, shall be subject to the penalties of this By-Law."

The penalty for not having a home or for depending on the generosity of others to get by was $100 (about $2350 in today's money) and up to two months in jail. It's not clear how those breaking the bylaw were expected to come up with the money to pay the fine if they didn't even have the cash to support themselves.

Good Fences Make Good Neighbours

Long gone were the days when livestock could legally roam wherever they wished, but that didn't keep the cows and other critters on their owner's property when there was no fence to pen them in. It got to be enough of a problem in Surrey that the city council appointed three men in 1884 to be official "fence viewers." The council also adopted a bylaw the next year to require the proper fencing of real property within the city limits. This bylaw made it the fence viewers' job to encourage the building and inspection of fences. They were also to mediate and, whenever possible, settle boundary disputes between neighbours.

Foreigners

British Columbia is a land of immigrants; over a quarter of its residents were born outside Canada. But the province has not always welcomed people of other lands.

LANGUAGE AND LAND

Immigration

The British North America Act of 1867 gave the provinces the power to regulate immigration into their respective jurisdictions as long as the local laws were not repugnant to any act of the Canadian Parliament.

The Legislative Assembly in 1900 mandated that all foreign immigrants settling in BC had to be able to fill out an application (the wording of which was laid out in the statute's provisions) "in the character of some language of Europe." Two years later, the legislature added the requirement that the immigrant had to be able to read "any test" submitted to them by one of various government officials. And finally, in 1905, a statute was enacted that prohibited any foreign immigrant who "fails to write out at dictation, in the characters of some language of Europe, and sign in the presence of the officer, a passage of 50 words in length, in an European language directed by the officer."

The law did not require the officer to ask for the passage to be written in English or French. Hopefully BC's immigration officers did not require it to be written in Gaelic (after all, a lot of BC's early residents were from Scotland) or something obscure like Switzerland's Rumantsch language.

The penalty for staying in BC after failing to write the 50-word passage was six months in jail and deportation. However, the wife or children under 18 of an immigrant who was already in British Columbia were exempted from having to write the passage.

Do You Own the Land You're Mining?

One of the legal concepts that BC inherited from Great Britain was that foreigners could not acquire, own or sell land. The idea came from the fact that aliens do not owe any allegiance to the Crown from whom, in theory, the title to all real estate is derived.

However, by late 1858, thousands of miners from the United States and other countries were working gold claims along the Fraser River. Soon thereafter, even more foreigners were buying and selling homes, farms, stores, hotels and other real estate throughout British Columbia. BC could easily have faced a legal nightmare if these folks did not actually have title to their land. (It wouldn't have encouraged settlement very much either.) So in September 1858, Governor James Douglas granted British Columbia's new residents permission to occupy their land for three years. However, at the end of that time, these aliens had to either become naturalized British subjects or convey the property to a British subject; otherwise, their land would be forfeited to the government. (Remember, there was no such thing as "Canadian citizenship" yet.)

An Addendum
The legislature of the United Colony of Vancouver Island and British Columbia went one step further by adopting the Alien's Ordinance in 1867. That law gave every alien in BC the right to "take, hold, enjoy, recover, convey and transmit" title to land just as if they were "natural-born British subjects" without ever having to obtain citizenship.

Taxes

*We all have to pay taxes, but that wasn't always true.
And how much you had to pay in the past, what you
were taxed on, and how you could fulfill your obligation
might surprise you.*

PROVINCIAL TAXES

Everything is Taxable

An 1876 provincial statute declared that all land, personal property and income in British Columbia was taxable by the City of Victoria. The specific tax rates were one-third of one percent of the assessed value of real estate; one-fifth of one percent of the assessed value of a person's personal property; and one-half of one percent of the income of every person making $1500 or more (or nearly $30,000 or more in today's money) per year.

There were a lot of land speculators in BC at the time who bought large tracts and then just let the property lie idle, so there was also a "Wild Lands Tax" of five cents on every unoccupied acre of land (which was defined as having no resident settler and $2.50—about $50 today—or less of improvements per acre) within the province.

Tax Breaks

There were numerous exceptions to the 1876 tax law.

For example, real estate within the province owned by either the federal or British governments could not be taxed. (Don't forget, BC and Canada were still very much part of the British Empire then.) Neither could any school, church, public library, courthouse, jail or public hospital be taxed, including the land they were situated on. The salaries of any soldiers or sailors stationed in British Columbia were also exempted as well as any pensions paid by the Canadian or British government to a BC resident.

The property and income of convicted prisoners, institutionalized lunatics and clergymen were non-taxable. Household effects "of whatever kind," as well as books, clothes and money invested in gold mines were also exempt.

No taxes were laid on a person's personal property if its net value was under $300. Likewise, all personal and real property, up to the value of any debts owed on the property (like a mortgage), were exempt.

Finally, the first 160 acres (65 hectares) of land if located west of the Cascades, and the first 320 acres (130 hectares) if east of the Cascades, were not taxed if they were actually occupied by a settler.

Provincial Income Tax

The 1876 income tax was not a graduated one. If your earnings for the year were only $1499.99, then you paid nothing, but add one penny and you suddenly owed one-half of one percent of your earnings, or $7.50.

Provincial Poll Tax

One of the earliest sources of revenue for the provincial government was a $3 head tax (about $65 today) that was placed in 1881 on every man in British Columbia who was 18 years of age or older. Your boss paid the tax if you were employed, but he also had the right to deduct the amount from your wages. Clergymen were exempted from paying the tax.

MUNICIPAL TAXES

Municipal Poll Tax

The province wasn't the only level of government that figured out that a head tax was a good way to raise revenue.

For example, the Township of Langley adopted a bylaw in 1907 requiring every male resident between the ages of 21 and 50 to pay a road tax of $2 per year. The top age was increased 10 years later to 60. And in 1940, the township replaced the road tax with a poll tax that required every male resident who was 21 or older and who was not already paying property taxes to pitch in $5 every year to the municipality. Women were excluded from these taxes.

Work Off Your Taxes

One of the first bylaws adopted by Surrey, in 1880, allowed local residents to pay off up to one half of their municipal taxes by working on road crews. They were paid $1.50 a day (approximately $33 today) for a 10-hour day and they had to supply their own tools (axes, shovels, etc.)

Library Dues

A 1936 bylaw in the Township of Langley required all local landowners, and all residents between 21 and 65 years of age who did not own land, to pay an annual tax of 65 cents toward the maintenance of the local library.

Voting

Democracy often takes some rather strange forms. Many wacky ideas, from keeping half of the residents from voting to outlawing polling and the distribution of campaign buttons and ribbons on election day, have been the law in BC at one time or another.

GOING TO THE POLLS

You Can't Vote in BC!

British Columbia was the first province to pass legislation expressly denying people the vote on the basis of race.

An 1872 law stated that, to be eligible to vote in a provincial election, you had to be male, a British subject, a 12-month resident of BC and at least 21 years of age. But the statute also said that "Nothing in this Act shall be construed to extend to or include or apply to Chinese or Indians." An 1876 law made it even clearer:

> *No Chinaman or Indian shall have his name placed on the register of voters for any electoral district, or be entitled to vote at any election of a member to serve in the Legislative Assembly of this Province.*

Furthermore, anyone who put a Chinese Canadian or Native name on the provincial voter's list faced a fine of up to $50 (almost $1000 today) or one month in jail.

Japanese Canadians were similarly denied the vote in 1895, as were "Hindus" (i.e., people of East Indian descent regardless of their religious affiliation) in 1907. Other legislation kept these ethnic groups from voting in municipal and school board elections.

These weren't just some barely-seen minorities who were being disenfranchised. According to the 1871 census, the First Nations made up nearly 71 percent of the province's population. They were still in the majority in 1881 and represented over one-quarter of the province's population in 1891. Likewise, in 1870, 15 percent of BC's non-Native population was of Chinese descent, and the percentage was much higher in places like Hope, Lytton, Yale and the Kootenays. In 1881, nearly one-fifth of Victoria's adult male population was Chinese. And between 1901 and 1931, Canadians of Chinese, Japanese and "Hindu" descent made up 10 percent of the province's population.

Wrong Religion Too!

The Doukhobors, Hutterites and Mennonites were denied the vote in BC's elections during the first half of the 20th century. The main reason was their objection to military service. Remember, thousands of British Columbians were killed during the two world wars, and pacifism was not very popular. The fact that the Doukhobors and Hutterites practiced communal farming didn't help their cause much either; everything that smacked of "collective" ownership of property was distrusted and feared. And the Doukhobors' nude protests against sending their kids to public schools did not win them many friends.

Must Know English or French

People without an "adequate knowledge" of English or French were denied the right to vote in British Columbia from 1947 to 1982. The prohibition was introduced the same year that the ban against voting by Chinese Canadians was repealed, so many saw it just as another attempt to keep British Columbians of Chinese descent away from the ballot box.

Who Else Couldn't Vote?

Schoolteachers were prohibited from voting in BC from 1878 to 1883. Others who have been denied the right to vote at some point in the province's history include provincial civil servants, judges, magistrates, police, soldiers, sailors, conscientious objectors and anyone working for the federal government (except postal employees).

Don't Have To Be Canadian!

Until 1985, all British subjects who lived in Canada for at least 12 months and in BC during the six months immediately before a provincial election were entitled to cast a ballot even if they weren't Canadians.

The federal Canadian Citizenship Act of 1946 created, effective January 1, 1947, a distinctive Canadian citizenship. Before then, Canadians were basically only British subjects who happened to live in Canada, legally speaking. Therefore, BC permitted everyone to cast a ballot in a provincial election (except those who were otherwise disqualified from voting) if they were "entitled within the Province to the privileges of a natural-born British subject" and met the above residency requirements.

The phrase "Canadian citizen" was added to the provincial elections law in 1947. Now, aside from specific exceptions (see above), everyone who was "entitled within the Province to the privileges of a natural-born Canadian citizen or British subject" could vote in a provincial election.

The phrase "British subject" was finally removed in 1985. Until then, the citizens of the United Kingdom, as well as those of countries like Australia, New Zealand and the Bahamas that recognize Queen Elizabeth as their head of state, and republics like India, Pakistan and Kenya that are part of the Commonwealth, could vote in BC's provincial elections without first obtaining Canadian citizenship.

How Much Property Do You Have?

In the beginning, only men of substantial wealth could vote and hold public office in British Columbia.

For example, in the colonial election of 1856 on Vancouver Island, all voters were required to own at least 20 acres (8 hectares) of land free of all debts and other encumbrances. To be a candidate, you had to own at least £300 (roughly $30,000 to $40,000 today) worth of land.

Most of the 1000 British colonists on Vancouver Island were fur traders, clerks or other low-paid employees of the Hudson's Bay Company, and these requirements eliminated almost everyone from the electoral process. In fact, there were only about 50 qualified voters in the entire colony.

Yes, She Can! No, She Can't.
In 1873, British Columbia became the first province to permit women to participate in a municipal election. However, to be eligible to vote, a woman had to not only meet the same age, residence and property qualifications that were required of a man, but she also had to be a "feme sole," which meant that she had to be divorced, widowed or never married. No wives were allowed to vote.

CASE FILE
Short by Two Hours

The first woman elected to the Vancouver City Council was Helena Gutteridge in 1937. It was not Gutteridge's first attempt to achieve public office; she ran for city council the year earlier.

Only people who owned at least $500 of real property within Vancouver were eligible under the city charter to run for council in the 1930s. In addition, the candidates had to have their property registered under their name for at least six months prior to the deadline for the submission of their nomination papers. Gutteridge had to withdraw from the 1936 race when it was discovered that she missed the six-month requirement by a mere two hours.

Voting Machines

The use of voting machines, instead of paper ballots, was first allowed in BC's municipal elections in 1900, but only on the approval of two-thirds of the municipal council of the locality where the machines were going to be used.

Who Are You Voting For?
The secret ballot was not introduced in British Columbia until 1873. Until then, in both BC's colonial elections and in its first provincial election in 1871, everybody had to appear before the local returning officer and verbally state loud enough for all bystanders to hear whom they were voting for.

No Treating Allowed

An 1896 provincial statute made it illegal for a candidate to directly or indirectly give a voter any meat, drink or other refreshment on the day of a municipal election. The crime was called "treating."

Oyez! Oyez! Oyez!

BC's election returning officers were legally required until 1940 to proclaim "Oyez! Oyez! Oyez!" at the start of every election day.

Oyez is a term that is often used to announce the opening of a court of law. It's a French word that dates from medieval England when French, rather than English, was the language of the country's aristocracy and upper class. The term means "hear ye" and is a call to silence.

No Cockades

It was unlawful in British Columbia until 1953 for a political candidate to provide any entertainment, music, buttons, flags, ribbons and cockades within eight days of an election.
(A cockade is a circular knot of ribbon, a rosette or a similar ornament that is usually worn on a hat.)

Must be Sober to Vote

A 1916 statute prohibited the sale of alcohol on the day of any municipal or provincial election.

The provision was originally meant to last only for the duration of World War I, which ended in 1918. However, Prohibition came to BC in 1917 and, when it was repealed four years later, the ban on selling booze on election day became permanent.

It remained illegal to sell liquor anywhere in the province on election day until 1977.

We're Taking a Poll

Public opinion polls gauging the popularity of political parties and their candidates during a provincial election were prohibited in British Columbia from 1940 to 1982.

CASE FILE
Get My Name Right!

Future premier Amor De Cosmos was originally born with the moniker William Alexander Smith. The name "Bill Smith" was, well, plain and boring, so Smith had his named legally changed when he lived in California in 1854. (He said that he wanted a name that reflected what he loved the most: "order, beauty, the world and the universe.")

De Cosmos arrived in Victoria in 1858 and was a candidate for the colonial legislature two years later. His political opponents had already once successfully argued that his name change was legal only in California, so De Cosmos was forced to run as "William Alexander Smith commonly known as Amor De Cosmos." There was no secret ballot yet, and every voter had to publicly announce the name of the person they were casting their ballot for. They also had to get their candidate's name right or their vote did not count. De Cosmos lost the election by only one vote when a person simply, but incorrectly, answered "Amor De Cosmos" when asked who his ballot was for.

Colonial BC

The British government granted Vancouver Island to the Hudson's Bay Company (HBC) in 1849 at the bargain-basement price of seven shillings per year. Today that would be only $42 per year!

The HBC, in turn, was expected to colonize the island within five years. The grant gave the company the power to sell land on the island to colonists at "a reasonable price" as well as to sell any coal or other minerals found (all for which the HBC got a 10 percent cut).

And the company had a money-back guarantee. The Imperial government reserved the right to recall the grant if the HBC failed to colonize the island. Furthermore, failure or not, the government could buy back Vancouver Island after 10 years provided it first reimbursed the company for whatever it spent to colonize the island as well as "the value of their establishments, property and effects then being thereon."

A NEW LAND

And Have We Got a Bargain for You!

The HBC issued a prospectus for potential colonists shortly after it received the grant to Vancouver Island. There were a number of conditions, however, before the company would sell you any land.

First, no Americans or other foreigners allowed! Only those who were "from Great Britain or Ireland, or from any other part of her Majesty's dominions" were welcome.

Second, land would be sold in lots of no less than 20 acres (8 hectares). The price, to be paid in cash at the HBC's headquarters in London, was £1 per acre (or about $120 in today's money), but even that was beyond the means of most people in 1849. The rich, however, could acquire larger tracts at the same £1-per-acre price if they brought with them to Vancouver Island five single men or three married couples for every 100 acres (40 hectares) they purchased.

Third, passage to Vancouver Island was at the colonists' expense.

Finally, any valuable minerals found on your land belonged to the HBC, though you'd be compensated for any damages suffered while the company dug. Also, if you discovered coal on your property, you could shovel it up yourself for a mere two shillings and sixpence per ton payable to the HBC.

Under these generous terms, you'd expect a flood of settlers to come to Vancouver Island, right? Actually, the only land sale for the first two years was to W.C. Grant in 1849. A former captain of the Second Dragoon Guards (aka the Scots Greys), Grant brought, at his own expense, eight other colonists with him to work on his property near Sooke Harbour.

Where's Your Mining Licence?

In May 1858, a few months before the colony of British Columbia was established, Vancouver Island's governor, James Douglas, visited the mining camps along the Fraser River. Douglas discovered during that trip that the miners at Hill Bar (near present-day Hope) had already established their own mining regulations. For example, they had determined that a mining claim would consist of a lot with a 25-foot (7.5-metre) frontage along the Fraser River.

The idea that the miners could make their own law was abhorrent, radical and unnatural to Douglas. It was also regarded as a sign that, if action wasn't taken soon, these miners (most of whom were Americans) might think that British law did not apply to BC's mainland and arrange for the United States to take over.

So Douglas quickly established his own mining regulations. A standard licence cost a miner 21 shillings and gave him title to a claim for square tract of land of 12 feet (3.5 metres) by 12 feet. Two miners working as partners would get a rectangular plot 12 feet by 24 feet (7 metres); three miners working together would get 18 feet (5.5 metres) by 24 feet; and four miners would get a claim 24 feet by 24 feet. No larger claims were allowed.

Furthermore, a miner had to keep the licence on his person at all times ready for inspection. And, of course, no mining was allowed on Sundays.

Early Business Licence Fees

After the Fraser River Gold Rush started in 1858, businessmen soon arrived to open saloons, hotels, stores and other establishments near the gold camps. These enterprises were usually housed in temporary buildings or tents. Regardless of the accommodations, everyone who carried on such an undertaking had to pay 30 shillings a month to the colonial government for the use of the land they occupied.

What a Way to Live

When William Duncan decided in 1862 to establish a mission for Natives at Metlahkatlah, he laid out some regulations for those who would live there.

First, the residents had to give up "the Demoniacal Rites called Ahlied or Medicine Work," including the use of "Shamans' or medicine men" and all other "heathen practices" to take care of the sick.

The Natives also had to stop "giving away property for display; [and] tearing up property in anger or to wipe out disgrace." (Duncan is presumably talking about the potlatch ceremony.) Mission residents were also required to be "cleanly in habits…be industrious…peaceful and orderly [and] be honest and upright in dealing with each other and indians [sic] of other tribes."

Other things the First Nations people at Metlahkatlah had to do include the following:

- stop gambling
- stop painting their faces
- stop drinking alcohol
- rest on the Sabbath
- attend religious instruction
- send their children to school
- build neat houses
- cultivate a garden
- pay the village tax

Triangular Lots

As governor of the mainland colony of British Columbia, James Douglas issued a proclamation in 1860 that gave every British subject the right to pre-empt (claim) up to 160 acres (65 hectares) of land. (Forget the First Nations who were already there; their title to the land wasn't recognized by the government.)

All a person had to do was erect a post at one corner of their claim and file a description of the land with the Chief Commissioner of Lands and Works and the property was theirs!

All plots had to be in the shape of a rectangle, and the width of each plot had to be at least two-thirds as long as its length. However, there was nothing in the proclamation about the direction of the lines; they could run east, west, north, south or whatever the pre-emptor wanted.

A new proclamation was issued by Douglas in 1861 requiring the survey lines to run north and south along the cardinal points of the compass unless the boundaries of some previously located claims or some natural feature (such as a lake or river) were used instead. To fit the new claims established under this decree in between those already staked out according to the 1860 proclamation, some rather irregularly shaped land claims resulted, including triangles!

Miscellaneous

The list of topics that one can write a law for is endless. From the correct way to draw a city map to how many of your friends you can meet in a public place, somebody somewhere and at sometime has enacted a statute or bylaw to regulate the activity. Most of these laws (though not all) have good intentions behind them, but several also had some rather odd, or even bizarre, results.

CONTROLLED SUBSTANCES

No Evidence that You're Guilty—but You've Still Got to Pay

Mission adopted a bylaw in 2009 that allows its fire safety inspectors to go into your home without your permission to look for marijuana grow operations if BC Hydro reports that you're using an abnormally high amount of energy. If the inspectors find a grow-op, they call the police—who have usually accompanied them and are waiting at the curb. (Without the inspectors' say-so, the cops would need some other reason to believe that an illegal activity was happening before they could enter your premises. They'd usually require a search warrant, too.)

Mission is not alone; nine other communities (Abbotsford, Chilliwack, Coquitlam, Langley, Langley City, Pitt Meadows, Port Coquitlam, Richmond and Surrey) have similar bylaws. But what makes Mission unique is that, even if no evidence of a grow-op is found, you are charged $5200 for the inspectors' time. And some of those inspections take only 10 or 15 minutes! People doing nothing more than heating their pool or running their hot tub have found an inspector at their door and a bill in their mail. To date, Mission has collected over $1 million from these inspection fees.

(Note: British Columbia enacted the Safety Standards Act in 2006 to allow municipal fire safety inspectors, with police escorts, to enter a dwelling without a search warrant to check for grow-ops. The BC Court of Appeals ruled in 2010 that the presence of the cops during the search without a warrant violates the Charter of Rights. That's why the police now wait at the curb.)

No Tobacco Ads

It was illegal for a short time to advertise tobacco products in British Columbia. The Tobacco Advertising Restraint Act of 1971 prohibited all publishing, distribution and broadcasting of tobacco advertising except at the point of sale.

The tobacco companies naturally objected and went to the BC Supreme Court to complain, but they lost. They were planning to appeal, but then the Legislative Assembly repealed the statute in 1972 and replaced it with the Tobacco Products Act, which permitted advertising with certain restrictions (such as requiring warning labels on tobacco products).

ONLY THE RIGHT TYPE OF PEOPLE CAN GATHER HERE

The Wobbly Effect

Vancouver was afraid in 1912 of the Wobblies (i.e., members of the union known as the Industrial Workers of the World), so it outlawed all public gatherings of more than three people. The city also banned the making of any speeches in parks, on sidewalks or on other public property.

Remember, Three's a Crowd

It was once against the law in Vancouver to simply be a part of a crowd. Specifically, a 1919 Vancouver bylaw made it illegal "…for any persons to collect in crowds or, by congregating thereon or therein, to obstruct any public place, or to refuse to disperse when so congregated, upon being requested to do so by any police officer."

It was also illegal to be "one of such crowd or congregation" or to "attract the persons and cause them to congregate upon and obstruct any public place." No definition was given as to how many people constituted a crowd.

No Hippies at the Fountain!

A beautiful mosaic fountain was installed in 1966 in front of what is now the Vancouver Art Gallery. (At the time, the building housed the city's main courthouse.) The fountain and the immediately surrounding area were meant as spaces for the public to rest, relax and enjoy the scenery, or to pass the time idly, to loaf around, to dawdle. Or, in other words, to loiter.

On the afternoon of March 9, 1968, approximately 200 people were doing just that. But then the Vancouver police arrived. They had supposedly received complaints from provincial government officials (whom they refused to name) and so they arrested 17 people between the ages of 19 and 27 for "unlawfully loitering on the areas appurtenant to a government building, to wit, the Court House, 800 block West Georgia" in violation of the Public Works Act. The police had with them a number of "John Doe" warrants that neither named nor described the people they were suppose to arrest. Also, while the maximum penalty for loitering was only $25, the bail set for all of the defendants was $50! (That's more than $300 today.) It was later discovered that the bail amount had been decided upon days in advance of the arrests.

And how did those 17 people differ from the others who were enjoying the fountain? All of them were young. But more importantly, most (but not all) did not conform to the prevailing style of dress and behaviour. In other words, they were hippies.

CITIES AND STREETS

Surrey Is the Biggest!

The Township of Langley was incorporated in 1873 and
Surrey six years later. BC's Municipal Act of 1872 provided
that no incorporated city, town or village within the province
could be larger than 100 square miles (259 square kilometres).
However, someone made a mistake when they drew Surrey's
original boundaries and left a strip about one-half mile
(2.5 kilometres) wide between it and Langley. A poll of the
residents within the strip found that a majority preferred to
be a part of Surrey and so the strip was annexed to the
municipality in 1882, making Surrey the largest municipality
in British Columbia (geographically speaking) at the time.

City of South Vancouver

South Vancouver was a separate city from 1892 until it
became part of Vancouver in 1929. South Vancouver's residents voted 1914 to 200 in 1911 in favour of annexation to
their neighbour to the north. However, the provincial government said "no." According to Victoria, Vancouver already had
too many problems of its own and didn't need to add South
Vancouver's to it.

Honour More Battles!

The Vancouver City Council decided in 1906 that more local
streets needed to be named after famous battles. As a result,
Campbell Street became Alma Street (after the Crimean War
fight) and Richards became Balaclava ("Remember the Light
Brigade!").

Vancouver already had two streets named Cornwall, so one
was renamed Blenheim (a 1704 battle in the War of the
Spanish Succession). And likewise, Lansdowne became
Waterloo and Boundary became Trafalgar after those two
decisive victories during the Napoleonic Wars.

TIDBITS

Ban-happy

Pitt Meadows has been described as the "ban-happy capital of Canada" by the Globe and Mail. The community has bylaws against strip joints, used car lots and home-based businesses. It also prohibits massage parlours, X-rated video stores, hydroponic retail outlets and nuclear power plants. And there's a ban against giant advertisements on top of buildings.

No Sympathy for the Deformed

An 1896 Nanaimo bylaw made it illegal for "any malformed, deformed or diseased person [to] expose himself or be exposed in any street or public place in order to excite sympathy or induce help."

No Snowball Fights

Esquimalt was incorporated in 1912. One of its first bylaws (number nine, to be exact) stated that "no person shall use any bow or arrow, catapult [sic] or sling-shot, or throw any stones, snowballs or other missiles within the limits of the Municipality."

Turn Off Those Lights

It was wartime and Vancouver held its first city-wide blackout for 15 minutes between 10:00 and 10:15 pm on May 22, 1941. Failure to turn out your lights could cost you a $500 fine (over $7000 today) and a year in jail.

What Time Is It?

The residents of northeast and southeast British Columbia voted overwhelmingly in 1972 to reject Daylight Saving Time (DST). In effect, they opted out of the provincial law that made DST uniform across BC and left the decision as to when to set their watches to the local municipalities.

BC became the first province to adopt DST (in 1919), but it wasn't always popular with everyone. In fact, DST barely survived a province-wide referendum in 1952 when rural communities like Chilliwack, Delta, Prince Rupert and Surrey voted overwhelming for its repeal, and only large majorities in Vancouver and Victoria kept it alive.

Today, in the northeast corner of the province, time stands still all year round in the communities of Chetwynd, Dawson Creek, Fort St. John, Hudson's Hope, Mackenzie and Tumbler Ridge. The citizens there do not have to remember "spring forward, fall back," because they are in the Mountain Time Zone, along with neighbouring Alberta, during winter and in the Pacific Time Zone, with the rest of BC, in summer.

Creston and Yahk in the East Kootenays also ignore DST and follow Mountain Time in winter and Pacific Time in summer. The rest of the East Kootenays, from Cranbrook to Golden and including Elkford, Fernie, Invermere, Kimberley and Sparwood, follow Mountain Time (i.e., Alberta time) all year round.

No Nukes Here

The voters in Smithers have passed a referendum declaring their town a Nuclear Weapons Free Zone.

Laundry

A 1913 Vancouver bylaw prohibited any laundry from being built or doing business within 200 yards (180 metres) of the Vancouver City Hall or of any public school, church, hospital or courthouse.

Build Us a Road

British Columbia enacted a statute in 1881 requiring all men in the province who were 18 or older who lived within a municipality (i.e., an incorporated city, district or town) to provide up to two days of free "statute labour" every year to their community or pay $1.50 per diem (about $33 today) to get out of it. That way, the municipalities had the workforce needed to build roads, sewers and other civic improvements. Someone must have complained because the law was substantially altered 10 years later.

First of all, only those living in a "town or district municipality" now had to provide statute labour; those residing in cities (like Vancouver and Victoria) were exempted.

Second, if the project was the construction or repair of a road or highway, only men between the ages of 21 and 50 were expected to show up.

Finally, for all other civic projects, everyone—male and female, resident and non-resident—who owned real property that was listed on a municipality's tax rolls had to donate some amount of their time to the community. This was apparently in addition to any roadwork they were required to do.

An entire schedule was created to determine how much work a property owner had to contribute. If your real estate was assessed at $500 or less, you owed two days of free statute labour every year. If it was worth more than $500, but less than $1000, you owed three days of work. If it was valued at between $1000 and $2000, you owed four days, and for every $1000 above $2000, you were expected to donate one additional day of your time.

The 1891 amendment gave municipal councils the discretion of paying for your mileage to and from the worksite. The councils were also given the power to set a sum, not exceeding $2 for every day of labour expected, that you could pay if you wanted to get out of your civic obligation.

Can You Spare a Body?

A statute enacted by British Columbia's colonial legislature in 1869 decreed that the bodies of anyone "found dead," "publicly exposed" or who immediately before their passing had been a patient at a public hospital while receiving financial aid from the colony, were to be impartially distributed among the colony's physicians "who may require such bodies for dissection, either for their own improvement or the instruction of any Student or Students under them." (There was no medical school in BC at the time.) Doctors who availed themselves of the "benefits" of this law had to post a $100 bond with the colony's Medical Registrar to ensure the proper burial of the remains once the dissection was completed. It beat grave robbing, which was common practice at the time to obtain human cadavers for medical training.

Of course, the bodies were not handed over for dissection if the deceased had given other instructions or if their family or friends claimed the body within "the usual period for interment."

No Baby Carriages on the Sidewalk
Prince George adopted a bylaw in 1929 allowing pedestrians to require a person pushing a baby carriage to step aside so they can pass or, if there's not enough room, to take the carriage off the sidewalk.

ABOUT THE ILLUSTRATORS

Peter Tyler

Tyler is a recent graduate of the Vancouver Film School's Visual Art and Design and Classical Animation programs. Though his ultimate passion is in filmmaking, he is also intent on developing his draftsmanship and story-telling, with the aim of using those skills in future filmic misadventures.

Roger Garcia

Roger Garcia immigrated to Canada from El Salvador at the age of seven. Because of the language barrier, he had to find a way to communicate with other kids. That's when he discovered the art of tracing. It wasn't long before he mastered this highly skilled technique, and by age 14, he was drawing weekly cartoons for the *Edmonton Examiner*. He taught himself to paint and sculpt, and then in high school and college, Roger skipped class to hide in the art room all day in order to further explore his talent. Currently, Roger's work can be seen in a local weekly newspaper and in places around Edmonton.

ABOUT THE ILLUSTRATORS

Patrick Hénaff

Born in France, Patrick Hénaff is mostly self-taught. He is a versatile artist who has explored a variety of media under many different influences. He now uses primarily pen and ink to draw, and then processes the images on computer. He is particularly interested in the narrative power of pictures.

Djordje Todorovic

Djordje Todorovic is an artist/illustrator living in Toronto, Ontario. He first moved to the city to go to York University to study fine arts. It was there that he got a taste for illustrating while working as the illustrator for his college paper *Mondo Magazine*. He has since worked on various projects and continues to perfect his craft. Aside from his artistic work, Djordje devotes his time to volunteering at the Print and Drawing Centre at the Art Gallery of Ontario. When he is not doing that, he is out trotting the globe.

ABOUT THE ILLUSTRATORS

Roly Wood

Roly Wood has worked in Toronto as a freelance illustrator, and has been employed in the graphic design department of a landscape architecture firm. In 2004, he wrote and illustrated a historical comic book set in Lang Pioneer Village, near Peterborough, Ontario. To see more of Roly's work, visit www.rolywood.com.

Graham Johnson

Graham Johnson is an Edmonton-based illustrator and graphic designer. When he isn't drawing or designing, he...well...he's always drawing or designing! On the off-chance you catch him not doing one of those things, he's probably cooking, playing tennis or poring over other illustrations.

ABOUT THE AUTHOR

Mark Thornburn

Mark Thornburn loves history and is the author of the
bestsellers, *Bathroom Book of British Columbia History*
and *British Columbia Place Names*. He has contributed to and
edited several history textbooks and references and has written for newspapers all across North America. Mark has lived
life as a lawyer and college instructor as well as a historian
and writer. He has a broad educational background, with
a BA in political science, a law degree and MAs in both
Canadian and American history. In his free time, Mark reads
great books, goes to the theatre, watches classic movies and
listens to Celtic music. He also likes hanging out at some of
the Vancouver's well-known spots, including Gastown,
Granville Island, Robson Street and Stanley Park.